TEST MATCH SPECIAL QUIZ BOOK

Dan Waddell

BBC
BOOKS

1 3 5 7 9 10 8 6 4 2

BBC Books, an imprint of Ebury Publishing
20 Vauxhall Bridge Road,
London SW1V 2SA

BBC Books is part of the Penguin Random House group of companies whose
addresses can be found at global.penguinrandomhouse.com

Penguin
Random House
UK

This book is published to accompany the radio series entitled *Test Match Special*
broadcast on BBC Radio 4 and 5 Live Sports Extra.

Head of BBC Radio Sport: Ben Gallop
Commissioning Editor: Richard Maddock
BBC Cricket Producer: Adam Mountford

First published by BBC Books in 2016

www.penguin.co.uk

A CIP catalogue record for this book is available from the British Library

ISBN 9781849908726

Illustration: Pete Ellis www.drawgood.com

Printed and bound in Great Britain by Clays Ltd, St Ives plc

Penguin Random House is committed to a sustainable future for our business, our readers
and our planet. This book is made from Forest Stewardship Council® certified paper.

MIX
Paper from
responsible sources
FSC
www.fsc.org
FSC® C018179

CONTENTS

INTRODUCTION

No sport inspires devotion quite like cricket. I've played and watched the game for more than 40 years, and during that time I've met men and women who know more about the game than they do about anything else. I've encountered people who can't remember the date they were married but can tell you without pause that Bob Willis bowled England to an improbable victory, after Ian Botham's heroic hundred, against Australia at Headingley on 21 July 1981; or who are unable to remember their A-level results, but can tell you that Donald Bradman's final Test batting average was 99.94.

For this reason, cricket, with its endless statistics, records, oddities and idiosyncrasies, is an ideal subject for a quiz book. And for the vast majority of modern cricket history, *Test Match Special* has borne witness and added lustre to all the great feats and moments in its rich, storied history. These 3000 questions (making this, at the time of writing, the most comprehensive cricket quiz book in history – see, I said we liked records!) cover all facets of the game, from Test matches to ODIs, T20 to the county game, while also dipping into the rich history of *TMS* itself. Those voices have been part of our lives for decades. We think we know them well. But just how well?

And as we all know, Aggers, Blowers, Tuffers, C.M.J., Johnners and all the rest of the *TMS* team over the years have revelled in the quirky and the esoteric. So as well as questions tough and easy on great players, famous matches and series, records and stats, expect questions on the more peculiar aspects of cricketing lore, including some highlights from when listeners wrote in to challenge the encyclopaedic mind of the late Bill Frindall, the Bearded Wonder. 'Flintoff has three Fs; Strauss has three Ss; Pietersen has three Es. But can you name the England Test player to have four of the same letter in his surnames?' asked one listener. Bearders knew the answer. Do you?

You'll find many questions like that to test your breadth of your knowledge, but also your dexterity. For example, which cricketer is an anagram of Coldly Evil? Or Fearful Pile. Elsewhere you'll be challenged on your knowledge of cricket quotes. We all know which England captain unwisely said he would make the West Indies 'grovel' (Tony Greig), but do you know which England fast bowler said: 'A cricket tour in Australia would be a most delightful period in one's life if one was deaf'?

Whether your cricket listening began with Arlott and Johnners or Aggers and Boycott, you'll find plenty here that you know or will have you scratching your head, from the Golden Age of Grace to the modern era of Alastair Cook, and all points in between.

The umpires are out there, the field is set, the bowler is marking his run. So take guard, allow time to get your eye in, and prepare for an enjoyable day of play.

PRE-MATCH CHAT

WARM UP

1. Which Australian fast bowler trod on a ball before the start of the second Ashes Test at Edgbaston in 2005 and missed the match?

2. Name the South African wicketkeeper who missed a match in the 2016 series against England after injuring his knee while walking his dogs.

3. Name the criminal in whose name protesters dug up the pitch at Headingley in 1975, so forcing the abandonment of the Test match between England and Australia.

4. At which ground in the West Indies was a Test match against England in 1998 cancelled after 10.1 overs when the pitch was deemed too dangerous for play?

5. Which extremely superstitious South African Test batsman insisted on putting all the lavatory seats down in the changing-room toilets before going out to bat?

6. Which successful Australian Test captain always carried a lucky red handkerchief in his pocket, given to him by his grandmother?

7.   Name the England all rounder who Aggers said 'failed to get his leg over' when he was out hit wicket against West Indies in 1991, causing legendary commentator Brian Johnson to corpse on air.

8.   Name the man who produced *Test Match Special* for 34 years between 1973 and 2007.

9.   In what year was the lbw law first introduced into the laws of cricket?

10.   Which English cricketer holds the record for the longest running Test match career, spanning 30 years, 315 days and 58 matches?

11.   What animal, killed by a cricket ball during play in 1936, is currently on display in the Lord's museum?

12.   What unusual event caused play to be stopped in a match between the Army and Royal Air Force in July 1944?

13.   In 1983 the Ashes Test match at Sydney was halted when a pig ran on the field, with the words 'Botham' and 'Eddie' painted on its side. What was the surname of 'Eddie', the English spinner to whom the name referred?

14.   Which song performed by Booker T and the MGs is played at the beginning and end of each *TMS* broadcast?

15. In what year was *Test Match Special* given its name?

16. Which nation was granted Test status in 2000?

17. Name the first Test player to be given out obstructing the field.

18. Two regular members of the *TMS* team have been given out Handled the Ball in Test matches. Name them.

19. The 1996 Test match at Trent Bridge between England and India was notable for the last time a long-running Test cricket tradition was observed in this country. What was it?

20. Which piece of equipment did England fast bowler Bob Willis forget to take out to the middle with him against Australia at Edgbaston in 1981?

NAME THE GROUND 1

1. Which ground has a Nursery End and a Pavilion End?

2. Which ground hosted its first Test match between England and Zimbabwe in 2003?

3. Which Test ground hosted the first ever Ashes Test to be held in England in 1884?

4. Which English Test ground is overlooked by a gasholder (gasometer)?

5. By what other name is the Brisbane Cricket Ground commonly known?

6. Which ground is unofficially believed to hold the record for the highest ever attendance at a Test match in 1999?

7. Which Test ground is also the headquarters of Yorkshire County Cricket Club?

8. Which county plays at the SWALEC Stadium?

9. Name the ground that held the first ever Test match in 1877.

10. At which ground did Peter May and Colin Cowdrey put on 411 against the West Indies, England's highest-ever partnership?

11. Which current Test ground has the lowest capacity?

12. In 2000, which ground saw all four innings of the match between England and West Indies played on the same day?

13. Which English ground hosted its one and only Test match between England and Australia in 1902?

14. Which English Test venue was a cabbage patch before it became a cricket ground?

15. The 1981 series between England and Australia became known as Botham's Ashes for the all rounder's match-winning feats at Headingley, Edgbaston and Old Trafford. But at which ground did England lose their only match of that series?

16. From a fort overlooking which ground in Sri Lanka was Aggers forced to cover the 2001 Test match after the BBC were locked out?

17. At which Test ground was the match between England and Australia abandoned without a single ball being bowled in 1938?

18. Which cricket ground is overlooked by Table Mountain?

19. Which English cricket ground, which hosted a match in the 1999 World Cup, was famous for having a tree on its outfield?

20. Which ground has an honours board in each dressing room listing all those who have scored a century or taken five wickets in every Test match played there?

NAME THE PLAYER 1

Name the players with these nicknames:

1.   The Master Blaster.

2.   The Rawalpindi Express.

3.   The Don.

4.   White Lightning.

5.   Pica.

6.   Beefy.

7.   Big Ship.

8.   Super Cat.

9.   The Cat.

10. The Master.

11. Tugga.

12. Little Master.

13. Bumble.

14. The Gaffer.

15. Big Bird.

16. Dizzy.

17. The Wall.

18. Creepy.

19. The Chef.

20. The King of Spain.

NAME THE COUNTY

Name the English county cricket sides the following men mainly played for:

1. David Gower.

2. John Emburey.

3. Martin Crowe.

4. Allan Lamb.

5. Andrew Flintoff.

6. Colin Dredge.

7. Brian Lara.

8. Leonard Hutton.

9. Wally Hammond.

10. Harold Larwood.

11.   Asif Iqbal.

12.   Shane Warne.

13.   Richie Richardson.

14.   Derek Randall.

15.   Colin Cowdrey.

16.   Ted Dexter.

17.   Basil D'Oliveira.

18.   Kim Barnett.

19.   Jim Laker.

20.   Matthew Maynard.

QUICK FIRE 1

1. Who won the first cricket World Cup in 1975?

2. Who has won the most Ashes Tests, England or Australia?

3. Name the missing dismissal: bowled, stumped, caught, lbw, stumped, run out, hit wicket, handled the ball, hit ball twice and timed out.

4. Who played in cricket's last timeless Test match in 1939?

5. How many World Cup finals have England lost?

6. In which country was Kevin Pietersen born?

7. Which Test nation did George Headley play for?

8. Which newspaper printed a spoof obituary which gave the Ashes their name?

9. To the nearest centimetre, how high is the Ashes urn?

10. Which two nations contested the first ever international cricket match?

11. Which was the last nation to be given Test status?

12. How many Tests have ended in a tied match?

13. Which all rounder became the first player to hit six sixes in an over in 1968?

14. Which nations hosted the 1996 World Cup?

15. What nationality is umpire Billy Bowden?

16. Name the cricketer who sparked an international furore when he delivered the last ball of the game underarm to prevent the opposition scoring the six they needed to win.

17. What did Ian Botham score in his match-winning Headingley knock in 1981?

18. In the same match, what odds against an England victory did Aussie players Dennis Lillee and Rod Marsh take?

19. Name the cricketing term used to describe a batsman being dismissed first ball in both innings of a match.

20. Give the full names of the two men whose mathematic formula helps calculate the winning target in rain-affected one-day matches.

WELCOME TO
TEST MATCH
SPECIAL

NAME THE COMMENTATOR

1. Which *TMS* commentator was known as 'The Boil'?

2. Which newspaper writer and commentator was known for his end of play summaries on *TMS* until he left the team in 1975?

3. Which commentator was christened 'The Alderman' by Brian Johnston?

4. Which former Middlesex and England fast bowler served as an expert summarizer between 1988 and 2008?

5. Name the great England fast bowler turned summarizer who often expressed bewilderment about what was 'going off' on the field of play.

6. Which commentator habitually greets guests and colleagues on air as 'My Dear old Thing'?

7. Who holds the record for being the longest serving *TMS* commentator, between 1973 and 2012?

8.   Name the female cricket commentator who made her *TMS* debut during the 2007 World Twenty20.

9.   Name the current *TMS* commentator who also goes under the name 'The Analyst'.

10.   Which famous *TMS* commentator's distinctive voice was once described as an 'articulate, leisurely, confiding countryman's burr'?

11.   Which *TMS* commentator's last commentary was the sixth Ashes Test in August 1993?

12.   Which former English captain joined the *TMS* team in 2009?

13.   Which overseas commentator made his *TMS* debut in 1966 and made regular appearances for almost 50 years?

14.   Which long serving statistician was affectionately known by his nickname 'The Bearded Wonder'?

15.   Which former Somerset spinner joined the *TMS* team in 1990?

16.   Which much loved *TMS* summarizer had his playing career curtailed by losing the sight in his left eye after a motoring accident in 1969?

17. Which current *TMS* summarizer used the phrase 'Feng Shui'd' to describe someone being bowled ('he's had his furniture rearranged...')?

18. Which *TMS* expert summarizer is fond of invoking his mother's catching ability to highlight the easiness of a missed chance?

19. Which current television commentator spent five years as a regular summarizer in the *TMS* box between 1990 and 1995?

20. Which broadcasting great, more commonly known for presenting cricket on BBC TV, commentated on two Test matches for *TMS* in 1958?

TRUE OR FALSE – *TMS*

1. Her Majesty the Queen once presented the *TMS* team with a cake.

2. Brian Johnston once said, 'The bowler's Holding, the batsman's Willey.'

3. Richie Benaud once enjoyed a brief stint as a *TMS* commentator.

4. Henry Blofeld was once described a butterfly on the pitch as having 'a limp'.

5. The first slogan for *TMS* in the *Radio Times* was 'Don't miss a ball, we broadcast them all'.

6. Fred Trueman once admitted on air that he bowled no faster than brisk medium pace.

7. Jonathan Agnew once grilled Marks and Spencer Executive Chairman Sir Stuart Rose about the price of bras.

8. Christopher Martin-Jenkins once mixed up his mobile phone with a TV remote.

9. Henry Blofeld once rapped live on the show with the Duckworth Lewis Method.

10. Ed Smith has a double first in history from Cambridge University.

11. Alison Mitchell played cricket for Northamptonshire.

12. Charles Dagnall attempted a career as a quarterback in American football.

13. Brian Johnston once referred to Trevor 'The Boil' Bailey as 'The Balls'.

14. Geoff Boycott once recited the Rudyard Kipling poem 'If' on air at the end of an Ashes Test match.

15. Phil Tufnell was once an extra in an episode of *EastEnders* propping up the bar of the Queen Vic.

16. Tom Cruise was once due to appear in the *TMS* box while on a promotional tour for *Mission: Impossible 2* but sadly had to cancel.

17. Fred Trueman once attempted a career as a stand-up comic.

18. Simon Mann is a fanatical supporter of Bristol Rovers FC.

19. Graeme Swann is the lead singer of a band named Dr Comfort and the Lurid Revelations.

20. Regular *TMS* guest summarizer and former New Zealand captain Jeremy Coney is also a trained stage lighting designer and once lit a play named *I Found My Horn*.

JOHNNERS
AND ARLOTT

1. John Arlott was once a policeman. True or false?

2. Of which batsman did Arlott use the description: 'The stroke of a man knocking a thistle top off with a walking stick'?

3. Who was Arlott describing when he said, 'On a ground where you've played some of the biggest cricket of your life and where the opposing side has just stood around you and given you three cheers, and the crowd has clapped you all the way to the wicket – I wonder if you really see the ball at all?'

4. For which first-class county did Arlott make a brief, sole appearance as a substitute fielder?

5. Which famous English cricketer became friends with Arlott and credits him with his lifelong love of wine?

6. Whose remarkable spell of spin bowling in 1956 did Arlott describe, with typical understatement, as 'very great piece of bowling'?

7. What word did Arlott employ to describe the first streaker in English cricket history?

8. Of which famous fast bowler did Arlott write a biography?

9. On which British island did John Arlott spend the last years of his life?

10. In which year did Arlott perform his last Test commentary for *TMS*?

11. What was Brian Johnston's middle name?

12. Name the long-running Sunday evening radio programme which Johnners presented for 15 years, between 1972 and 1987.

13. Which soap opera was Johnners a fan of?

14. Which Australian commentator did Brian Johnston christen 'The Doctor' because of his initials 'N.O.'?

15. Which medal was Johnners awarded for his service during the war?

16. In what year was Johnners made BBC cricket correspondent?

17. Complete this famous piece of commentary, 'Aggers, for goodness sake...'

18. Which major national event did Johnners commentate on in 1953?

19. Of which former England captain did Johnners utter this famous description: 'X has just relieved himself at the Pavilion End.'

20. In what year did Johnners die?

AGGERS AND BOYCOTT

1. Name the Yorkshire village where Boycott was born in 1940.

2. Against which country did Boycott make his Test debut in 1964?

3. Which item of clothing does Boycott often claim his mother could've caught the ball in?

4. What animal did Boycott confess to having as a pet as a boy during Aggers's *Mastermind* questions in 2012?

5. Who was the 'little wizard' Boycott threatened to turn into a mouse for asking an embarrassing question?

6. Off which bowler did Boycott strike a boundary to reach his 100th first-class hundred in front of his home crowd at Headingley in 1977?

7. Which politician revealed on *TMS* that he was in the crowd on that day?

8. Is Boycott's Test bowling average higher or lower than Aggers's?

9. Why was Boycott dropped from the England Test team after he scored 246 not out against India in 1967?

10. Boycott once played a handful of games for which football club's under 18s team?

11. Which school in Rutland did Aggers attend as a boy?

12. Which Lancashire batsman was 18-year-old Aggers's first first-class wicket on his debut for Leicestershire in 1978?

13. Against which side did Aggers make his Test debut in 1984?

14. Which batsman was his first Test victim?

15. In the 1987 season, which bowling feat did Aggers accomplish?

16. What illustrious cricketing accolade did the above feat win him?

17. In 1992, two years after he hung up his boots, Aggers came out of retirement to play a NatWest semi-final for Leicestershire against which county?

18. In ODIs, does Aggers have a lower or higher strike rate as a batsman than Boycott?

19. Which international tournament did Aggers present for BBC TV?

20. Although commonly known as Aggers, after which USA Vice President is he also nicknamed?

BEST OF BEARDERS 1

A selection of questions from the long-running section of the *TMS* website, 'Ask Bearders', where listeners wrote in to challenge Bill Frindall, the late *TMS* scorer.

1. True or false. Aggers once scored 76 for Leicestershire against Yorkshire as nightwatchman.

2. True or false. Warwick Armstrong weighed 22 stone at the end of his playing career.

3. True or false. Yorkshireman Bobby Peel was banned from the Yorkshire team in 1897 for taking the field drunk and urinating in front of Lord Hawke.

4. What is the highest number of runs scored by a player who was NEVER dismissed in Test cricket?
    a) 66
    b) 76
    c) 86

5. Who surpassed Bob Willis's record of 55 career not outs?

6. Flintoff has three Fs; Strauss has three Ss; Pietersen has three Es. But can you name the England Test player to have four of the same letter in his surname?

7. Who was the last man to be given out by Dickie Bird in his final Test match in 1996 between England and India?

8. Why is David Lloyd called Bumble?

9. If a batsman drops dead at the crease, should they be given out or not out?

10. Who contested the shortest Test match ever played in 1932, lasting just 5 hours and 53 minutes?

11. Billy Murdoch was a fine batsman and scored 200 in a Test. Why did he only play one Test for England?

12. True or false. In a mix up where both batsmen are stranded at one end of the wicket, the batsmen choose who is out.

13. True or false. If an umpire miscounts and a batsman is dismissed off the seventh ball of the over, the dismissal doesn't count.

14. The score is 8 for no wicket after the first over. This over consisted of four dot balls and then two run-scoring shots. At the end of the over both batsmen were on four not out. How?

15. When was the 'free hit' first introduced by the ECB as a penalty for no balls in limited overs matches?

16. True or false. Only a wicketkeeper can stump a batsman.

17. The batting side needs one run to win. The fielding side need one wicket to win. The fielding side bowl a wide but the batsman is stumped. Who wins, or is it a draw?

18. How many ways are there to get out in cricket?
    a) 8
    b) 9
    c) 10

19. True or false. Both batsmen can be run out off the same ball.

20. At which overseas ground have England won most Tests?

QUICK FIRE 2

1. *TMS* started on air in which year?

2. *TMS* was aired on which BBC radio station?

3. Since moving to Radio 4, *TMS* has been interrupted by which famous BBC broadcast?

4. Name the son of *TMS* stalwart C.M.J., who played first-class cricket for Sussex.

5. For which county did Simon Hughes play his entire first-class career?

6. Henry Blofeld had an exceptional schoolboy career for which famous school?

7. Vic Marks made his England debut in 1982 against which team?

8. For which national newspaper is former *TMS* summarizer Mike Selvey currently cricket correspondent?

9. Trevor Bailey shared a famous fifth wicket stand with which other cricketer to deny the Australians victory at Lord's in 1953?

10. What's the nickname given to former England opener and *TMS* summarizer Graeme Fowler?

11. Which Australian player was Fred Trueman's 300th Test victim?

12. Which woman became *TMS*'s first female commentator in 1998?

13. Occasional *TMS* summarizer Ravi Shastri played for which nation?

14. Former New Zealand wicketkeeper and *TMS* regular Ian Smith commentates on which other sport?

15. Who succeeded 'The Bearded Wonder' Bill Frindall as *TMS* scorer after his death in 2008?

16. Which Middlesex and England fast bowler made regular appearances as a summarizer on *TMS* between 2002 and 2008?

17. Which county did England spinner Graeme Swann leave to move to Nottinghamshire in 2005?

18. Alec Stewart is a fanatical fan of which English football club?

19. True or false. Yorkshire hero Michael Vaughan was actually born in Lancashire.

20. Which former *TMS* regular commentated on every Test in Australia from the Second World War until his retirement in 1985?

MEET
THE TEAMS

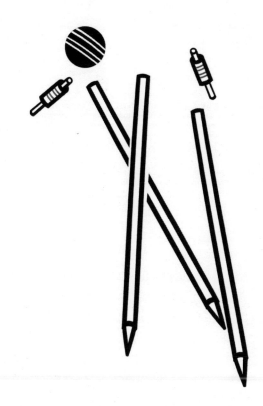

ENGLAND

1. Name England's highest run scorer in Tests.

2. Name England's highest wicket taker.

3. Who holds the record for highest English Test score?

4. Who holds the record for England's best bowling analysis in a single innings?

5. Name England's most capped player (at March 2016).

6. Which English wicketkeeper holds the record for his country's most Test-match catches?

7. Name England's longest serving Test-match captain (number of matches).

8. Who is England's most successful captain (number of victories)?

9. At which English ground have England played most Tests?

10. What is the lowest total England have been dismissed for in Test cricket?

11. Name the first non-white player to play for England.

12. Which English chairman of selectors famously referred to fast bowler Devon Malcolm as 'Malcolm Devon' in 1989?

13. In the 1988 summer England had four captains: Mike Gatting, Chris Cowdrey, Graham Gooch and which other?

14. Which Zimbabwean was appointed England coach in 1999?

15. Which English captain unwisely said he wanted to make the West Indies 'grovel' in 1976?

16. Which continent did the first English touring team visit?

17. Which player has the record for the fastest hundred scored by an English player in Test cricket (by balls faced)?

18. Name the first English bowler to claim a hat-trick in Test matches.

19. Name the umpire with whom England captain Mike Gatting had an onfield row in Faisalabad in 1987.

20. Which English captain caused controversy when a TV camera appeared to show him having dirt in his pocket?

AUSTRALIA

1. Name Australia's highest run scorer in Tests.

2. Name Australia's highest wicket taker.

3. Who holds the record for the highest Australian Test score?

4. Who holds the record for Australia's best bowling analysis in a single innings?

5. Name the two players who share the record of Australia's most capped player.

6. Which Australian wicketkeeper holds the record for his country's most Test-match catches?

7. Name Australia's longest serving Test-match captain (number of matches).

8. Who is Australia's most successful captain (number of victories)?

9. Who did Australia beat in February 2002 by an innings and 360 runs to complete their largest Test victory?

10. What is the lowest total Australia have been dismissed for in Test cricket?

11. Which Australian faced the first ball in Test cricket, scored the first half century and the first century?

12. Which of the Chappell brothers, Ian or Greg, had the best Test-match record as captain?

13. What is Dennis Lillee's middle name?

14. Which Australian captain broke down in tears when resigning in 1984?

15. Which swashbuckling Aussie all rounder was nicknamed Nugget?

16. Which Australian batsman was rumoured to have drunk 52 cans of beer on a flight to England?

17. Which Australian all rounder has a Test captaincy record of played one, lost one?

18. Which Australian cricketing legend was born in Penrith, New South Wales, in 1930?

19. By what name is the Australian Test cricket cap more commonly known?

20. Name the ground in Hobart, Tasmania, which is a Test-match venue.

INDIA

1. Name India's highest Test-match run scorer.

2. Name India's highest wicket taker in Tests.

3. Which player holds the record for highest Indian Test score?

4. Who holds the record for India's best bowling figures in a single innings?

5. How many Test matches did Sachin Tendulkar play?

6. Which Indian wicketkeeper holds the record for his country's most Test-match dismissals?

7. Name India's longest serving Test-match captain (number of matches).

8. Vinoo Mankad and Pankaj Roy hold the record for India's highest Test partnership. How much did they put on?

9. Which team bowled India out for 42 in 1974 for their lowest Test total?

10. In which year did India play its first Test match?

11. Which Indian batsman scored his nation's highest score on debut when he struck 187 v Australia at Mohali in 2013?

12. Which Indian batsman scored a match-winning 281 as India beat Australia at Eden Gardens in 2001 after being asked to follow on?

13. Which Indian Test batsman became only the second man in cricket history to hit six sixes in an over?

14. How many matches did it take India to record their first Test-match victory?

15. Against which Test nation did India win its first away Test series in 1967–8?

16. Which Indian all rounder scored 5248 Test runs and took 434 wickets?

17. Who was the Indian captain in 1971 when the team won back-to-back series victories against West Indies and England?

18. Which Indian cricketer is the only batsman in history to score a hundred in each of his first three tests?

19. Which Indian spinner was nicknamed 'The Turbanator'?

20. In which Indian city is the Wankhede Stadium?

PAKISTAN

1. Name Pakistan's highest Test-match run scorer.

2. Name Pakistan's highest wicket taker in Tests.

3. Which player holds the record for the highest Pakistan Test score?

4. Who holds the record for Pakistan's best bowling figures in a single innings?

5. Who is Pakistan's most successful Test captain?

6. Which Pakistani wicketkeeper holds the record for his country's most Test match dismissals?

7. Name Pakistan's longest serving Test-match captain (number of matches).

8. Which batsman holds the Pakistani record for the most half-centuries in Test cricket with 46?

9. Which Pakistani cricketer has been dismissed for a duck 25 times in his Test career?

10. In which year did Pakistan play its first Test match?

11. Which Pakistani batsman matched Viv Richard's record for the fastest ton in Test history v Australia at Abu Dhabi in 2016?

12. Against which nation did Pakistan play their first Test series?

13. Which batsman became the first Pakistani to score a double century at Lord's v England in 1982?

14. In what year did Pakistan play their last Test match on Pakistani soil?

15. Which two batsmen shared their nation's highest partnership of 451 against India in 1983?

16. Which fast bowler took 12 wickets when Pakistan completed a memorable victory over England at the Oval in 1952?

17. In which city, now the capital of Bangladesh, did Pakistan play their first home Test match in 1955?

18. Which Pakistani cricketer has the nickname 'Boom Boom'?

19. By what name was former Pakistani skipper Mohammad Yousuf known?

20. Who scored Pakistan's first Test-match century in 1952 and became the first Test player to stay on the pitch for the entire Test match?

SOUTH AFRICA

1. Name South Africa's highest Test-match run scorer.

2. Name South Africa's highest wicket taker in Tests.

3. Which player holds the record for highest South African Test score?

4. Who holds the record for South Africa's best bowling figures in a single innings?

5. Who is South Africa's most successful Test captain (most Test wins)?

6. Which South African wicketkeeper holds the record for the most Test-match dismissals of any nation?

7. Which team bowled South Africa out for 30 in 1896, their lowest Test-match total?

8. Jacques Kallis has scored the most Test centuries for South Africa. How many?

9. At which English ground did South Africa score their highest Test innings of 682-6 declared in 2003?

10. In which year did the ICC vote to suspend South Africa from international cricket for its government's policy of apartheid?

11. Who was the South African captain at the time of the ban?

12. Against which nation did South Africa play their first Test match back in 1992?

13. As a result of the ban, which South African batsman was restricted to playing only four Test matches at an average 72.57?

14. Which cricketer made their Test debut aged 40 on South Africa's re-entry to Test cricket in 1992?

15. Name Shaun Pollock's Test-playing father.

16. What do initials A.B. stand for in A.B. de Villiers's name?

17. Name the Test ground in Durban.

18. South African batsman Peter Kirsten enjoyed a successful career in 1978–82 for which English county?

19. South African Test cricketer Jonty Rhodes represented his country at which other sport?

20. Former South African captain Kepler Wessels played for which other Test nation?

WEST INDIES

1. Name the West Indies highest Test-match run scorer.

2. Name West Indies's highest wicket taker in Tests.

3. Who holds the record for the West Indies's best bowling figures in a single innings?

4. Clive Lloyd is the West Indies's longest serving captain. For how many matches was he in charge?

5. Which West Indian wicketkeeper holds his nation's record for most Test-match dismissals?

6. The West Indies's lowest Test match total came in 2004 when they were bowled out for 47 by which nation?

7. The West Indies's highest innings total came in 1958 v Pakistan when they declared on 790-3. Name the batsman who was undefeated on a then world record of 365.

8. Which West Indies bowler has the lowest Test bowling average?

9. Which West Indies batsman hold his nation's highest Test batting average?

10. Against which Test side do the West Indies have their lowest winning percentage?

11. West Indies great Brian Lara holds the record for the highest score in first-class cricket of 501, playing for which English county?

12. Which West Indies spinner became the first slow bowler to take 300 Test wicket and only the second in the game?

13. Which West Indian and Leeward Islands batsman was famed for batting in a wide-brimmed maroon hat rather than a helmet?

14. What was the name given by the media to the West Indies 5–0 defeat of England in 1984?

15. Name the West Indies batsman who scored a double century and a century on his debut.

16. In what year did West Indies win their first Test series in England?

17. Spinner Sonny Ramadhin was instrumental in that series. With which spin partner did he take 59 wickets?

18. Which West Indies bowler was given the nickname 'Whispering Death'?

19. Which West Indies batsman is the only player in history to hit the first ball of a Test match for 6?

20. Name the West Indies Test ground in Georgetown, Guyana.

NEW ZEALAND

1. Name New Zealand's highest Test-match run scorer.

2. Name New Zealand's highest wicket taker in Tests.

3. Which player holds New Zealand's record for highest Test score?

4. Against which nation did Richard Hadlee record his country's best bowling figures of 9-52 in 1985?

5. Name New Zealand's most successful Test captain (most Test wins).

6. Which New Zealand wicketkeeper holds his country's record for the most Test-match dismissals?

7. Which batsman holds New Zealand's record for the most centuries in Tests?

8. In 1955 at Auckland England bowled New Zealand out for their lowest total in Test history. What was that total?

9. Which successful opener top scored in this innings with 11?

10.   Which New Zealand batting 'rabbit' scored 36 ducks in his Test career?

11.   Name all rounder Richard Hadlee's cricketing brother.

12.   At which ground did New Zealand complete their first Test win in England in 1983?

13.   Which New Zealand batsman holds the record for the fastest double century in Test cricket?

14.   Which New Zealand player made his Test debut as captain v India in 1995?

15.   In what year did New Zealand play their first ever Test match?

16.   Against which team 25 years later did they win their first ever Test match?

17.   Name all rounder Chris Cairns's Test-playing father.

18.   With which other batsman did Martin Crowe put on a record partnership of 467 against Sri Lanka in 1991?

19.   By what nickname are the New Zealand cricket team commonly known?

20.   In which New Zealand city is the Test-match ground, Basin Reserve?

SRI LANKA

1. Name Sri Lanka's highest Test-match run scorer.

2. Name Sri Lanka's highest wicket taker in Tests.

3. Which player holds Sri Lanka's record for highest Test score?

4. Muttiah Muralitharan has taken nine-wicket Test hauls twice. Who is the only other Sri Lankan bowler to match the feat?

5. Name Sri Lanka's most longest serving Test captain.

6. Which Sri Lankan wicketkeeper holds his country's record for the most Test-match dismissals?

7. Which batsman holds Sri Lanka's record for the most runs scored in a Test series?

8. Against which nation in 1997 did Sri Lanka achieve their highest innings total of 952-6d?

9. Their two lowest totals of 71 and 73 were recorded against the same team on the same ground but 12 years apart. Name the team.

10. Who captained Sri Lanka against England in their first ever Test in Colombo in 1982?

11. Which batsman scored Sri Lanka's first Test century v Pakistan in 1982?

12. Sri Lanka won their first Test match in 1985. Against who?

13. Which spinner had match figures of 8-188 in Sri Lanka's first ever Test victory against England in 1993?

14. What is Sri Lanka's most successful all rounder Chaminda Vaas's full name?

15. Which Sri Lankan's batsman's first six Test innings yielded five ducks and a score of 1?

16. In which Sri Lankan city was Muttiah Muralitharan born?

17. Which former Sri Lankan batsman was elected to Parliament in the General Election of 2010?

18. Batting great Aravinda de Silva played for which English county in 1995?

19. The Sri Lanka Test team goes under what nickname?

20. The Sinhalese Sports Ground is in which Sri Lankan city?

BANGLADESH

1. Name Bangladesh's highest Test-match run scorer.

2. Name Bangladesh's highest wicket taker in Tests.

3. Which player holds Bangladesh's record for highest Test score?

4. Which Bangladeshi achieved the nation's best bowling figures of 8-39 v Zimbabwe in 2014?

5. Name Bangladesh's longest serving Test captain.

6. Against which nation were Bangladesh bowled out for 62 in 2007, their lowest total in Test cricket?

7. How many Tests did Bangladesh play before they won their first match?

8. Who did they defeat?

9. By what nickname is the Bangladesh cricket team commonly known?

10. Which former Australian cricketer coached Bangladesh in 2003–7?

11. Who is Bangladesh's highest run scorer in ODIs and also holds the record for their highest ODI score of 154?

12. Which player became the first Bangladeshi to score 2000 runs and take 100 wickets in ODIs?

13. Who scored Bangladesh's first ODI hundred against Zimbabwe in 1999?

14. Who became the first Bangladeshi cricketer to play for an English county when he signed for Worcestershire in 2010?

15. Who currently holds the record for most wickets in ODIs for Bangladesh with 207?

16. Who has the best figures in an ODI innings with 6-26 v Kenya in 2006?

17. Which player has played the most ODI matches for Bangladesh with 175?

18. Which Bangladeshi recorded a pair in his first Test as captain in 2004?

19. Who currently holds the record for most Test dismissals for a Bangladeshi wicketkeeper – Khaled Mashud or Mushfiqur Rahim?

20. Who is the current Bangladesh Test captain?

ZIMBABWE

1.   Name Zimbabwe's highest Test-match run scorer.

2.   Name Zimbabwe's highest wicket taker in Tests.

3.   Which player holds Zimbabwe's record for highest Test score?

4.   Which Zimbabwe bowler took 8-109 v New Zealand in 2000, his nation's best bowling figures in an innings?

5.   Name Zimbabwe's longest serving Test captain.

6.   By which nation were Zimbabwe bowled out for 52 in 2012, their lowest total in Test cricket?

7.   In which year did they play their first Test match?

8.   Who did they defeat in Harare by an innings and 64 runs in 1995 to claim their first Test victory?

9.   Zimbabwean brothers Grant and Andy Flower both played several seasons for which English county?

10.   Which fast bowler virtually ended his own international career by wearing a black armband to mourn the 'death of democracy' in his country in 2003?

11.   Who has second most runs in ODIs for Zimbabwe after Andy Flower?

12.   Who made their highest ODI score of 194 not out v Bangladesh in Bulawayo in 2009?

13.   Who has played most ODI matches for Zimbabwe?

14.   Who has taken second most wickets in ODIs after Heath Streak?

15.   Whose 6-18 against England in Cape Town 2000 remains the nation's best ODI figures?

16.   Who has been Zimbabwe's most economical bowler in ODIs?

17.   Ray Price is the nephew of which South African golfer?

18.   What year did Zimbabwe withdraw from playing Test matches?

19.   What year did they return?

20.   Which English county did Zimbabwe batsman Brendan Taylor play for in 2015?

DERBYSHIRE

1. When did the county play its first match?

2. Why did the county lose its first-class status in 1888?

3. When was their status reinstated?

4. What happened to Derbyshire in 1920?

5. When did Derbyshire win their one and only County Championship title?

6. Who was captain of that team?

7. Whose 140 wickets that season made him the country's leading bowler?

8. Two Derbyshire batsmen tied at the end of the season with 1322 runs. One was Stan Worthington. Name the other.

9. How was their home in Derby, now called the County Cricket Ground, formerly known?

10. Which other ground did they play at for 100 years, and have recently returned to?

11.	Which Derbyshire bowling legend, who criminally only played two Test matches, took 143 wickets in 1958 at an average of 10.99, a feat never bettered since?

12.	Who is the county's leading run scorer in first-class cricket?

13.	Which Australian scored 221 in the county's highest first-class score, 801-8 declared against Somerset at Taunton in 2007?

14.	Derbyshire won the Benson and Hedges Cup in 1993. Who did they beat in the final?

15.	Which all rounder scored 92 and was named man of the match?

16.	In 1981 the county beat Northamptonshire to win the first NatWest Trophy. In a thrilling finish, the scores were level. Why did Derbyshire win?

17.	Which New Zealand opener scored 76 to set up Derbyshire's run chase?

18.	Which off-spinning Derbyshire all rounder was selected for 34 Tests for England?

19.	Whose 84 wickets at 19.19 in 2014, the best for Derbyshire since 1984, earned him a call up to the England Performance Programme?

20.	What is the current limited overs name of the team?

DURHAM

1. In the 1973 Gillette Cup Durham became the first minor county to beat a first-class side. Who?

2. When did Durham join the County Championship?

3. Which ground hosted their first ever county match against Leicestershire in April of that year?

4. Who was their captain that year?

5. Which *TMS* commentator played that year, taking 34 wickets at 49.17 apiece?

6. Which Australian batsman topped the batting averages?

7. Which former Northamptonshire and England opener played for Durham between 1992 and 1995?

8. Which other Northamptonshire and England opener was the first director of cricket at Durham and went on to coach the club?

9. What year did Durham move to the Riverside Ground?

10. When did the Riverside Ground host its first Test?

11. When did Durham win promotion to the first division of the County Championship?

12. Which Australian was their captain for that successful season?

13. Which bowler in 1996 became the first Durham player to represent England?

14. In which year did Durham claim the first of their three County Championship titles?

15. Which Australian batsman scored 273 against Hampshire in 2003, the highest score in the county's first-class history?

16. Who is the highest run scorer in Durham's history?

17. Which West Indies bowler took all ten wickets for Durham against Hampshire in 2007?

18. Which seam-bowling stalwart holds the record for best match analysis, 15 for 95 against Northamptonshire in 2014?

19. What one-day tournament did Durham win in 2007, beating Hampshire in the final?

20. What is Durham's name in T20 cricket?

ESSEX

1. In what year did Essex join the County Championship?

2. How many times have they won the title?

3. In which town do they play most of their first-class matches?

4. In what year did they win their first County Championship?

5. Who was skipper for that year?

6. Which England captain led the county between 1911 and 1928?

7. Which England all rounder was the mainstay of the Essex post-war attack until his retirement in 1967?

8. What year did Graham Gooch make his debut for the county?

9. Which England left-arm seamer led the Essex attack for the 1970s and the 1980s?

10. Which overseas player played for Essex between 1974 and 1985, scoring more than a 1000 runs every season and scoring more than 2000 in 1983?

11. Which Essex all rounder and Cambridge graduate played 30 Test matches for England between 1982 and 1992?

12. Which long-serving Essex left-arm spinner was known as much for pranks and on-field wit as he was his bowling?

13. Who is Essex's all-time top run scorer with 30,701?

14. Who heads their list of bowlers with most first-class wickets with 1610?

15. Who scored their highest individual score of 343 not out v Derbyshire?

16. Which batsman shared Essex's record for first and second wicket partnerships with Graham Gooch?

17. Which Essex batsman captained his country for 45 Test matches?

18. Who did Essex defeat to win the Benson and Hedges Cup in 1979?

19. Graham Gooch won man of the match for his 120, but which West Indies quick's three wickets helped Essex to victory?

20. What is the name of Essex's limited overs team?

GLAMORGAN

1. What year did Glamorgan join the County Championship?

2. How many times has the county won the title?

3. Their main ground in Cardiff is on the banks of which river?

4. Where did Glamorgan play its first first-class match against Sussex in 1921?

5. How many games did the county win in their first season?

6. The county's first title came in which year?

7. Who was captain of that side?

8. What other sport did Glamorgan player Wilf Wooller play, appearing 18 times for Wales?

9. Which Glamorgan cricketer was called up to play for England v South Africa in 1935 but did not take a wicket, did not bat and did not play again?

10. Who was Glamorgan captain when they won their second County Championship in 1969?

11. Which dependable opener topped the county's averages that year, scoring 1441 runs?

12. Who was captain when they won the last of their three titles in 1997?

13. Who was coach of that title-winning side?

14. Which Pakistani bowler took 68 wickets at an average of 22.80 to help them to the title?

15. Who was responsible for Glamorgan's highest individual score when he struck 309 not out v Sussex in 2000?

16. Who is the county's all-time leading wicket taker with 2174?

17. How many Tests did Matthew Maynard play for England?

18. How many times has the team won the Sunday/National League?

19. Who is the current county captain?

20. What is the name of their limited overs team?

GLOUCESTERSHIRE

1.   Which cricketing family formed Gloucestershire in, it is believed, 1870?

2.   Who was the team's first captain?

3.   How many times has Gloucestershire won the official County Championship?

4.   In which city is the team's home ground?

5.   In which town does the county hold a famous cricket festival?

6.   Whose death from pneumonia in 1880 is said to have adversely affected the county for many years afterwards?

7.   Which legendary batsman scored 113 centuries for the county?

8.   W.G. Grace severed his connection with Gloucestershire in 1899 to go and form which short-lived first-class team?

9.   Which fast-scoring Gloucestershire and England batsman was known at the Croucher for his hunched stance at the crease?

10. Gloucestershire seamer Charlie Parker is third in the list of all-time first-class wicket takers with 3278. How many Tests did he play for England?

11. Which Gloucestershire off spinner, who started life as a seamer, sits fifth in the all-time first-class list of wicket takers with 2979?

12. Which stylish England batsman played for Gloucestershire between 1948 and 1960 before ending his career at Worcestershire?

13. Which New Zealand opener struck the county's highest individual score against Middlesex in 2004?

14. Who is the highest run scorer in their history with 33,664?

15. Which overseas player first played for the county in 1984 and was a mainstay of the side until 1998?

16. Which overseas all rounder played with great success for the county between 1965 and 1981?

17. Which Gloucestershire fast bowler's career was sadly cut short by a serious leg injury while bowling for England in 1992 against New Zealand?

18. Who did the county defeat in the 1999 NatWest Trophy final?

19. Who was made man of the match for his outstanding keeping in that final?

20. In 2013 Gloucestershire stopped using what as its limited overs name?

HAMPSHIRE

1. When did Hampshire join the County Championship?

2. In which city was the county's home ground until their move to the Rose Bowl in 2000?

3. How many times has the county won the County Championship title?

4. When was the first of those victories?

5. Who was the bold, swashbuckling captain who led them to that crown?

6. The grandson of which famous poet captained the side between 1919 and 1932?

7. Which left-handed batsman played for the county for 31 years between 1905 and 1936, scoring 48,892 runs, the highest in County Championship history and the most a player has ever scored for a single team?

8. Which white West Indies cricketer was the mainstay of Hampshire's batting between 1953 and 1972?

9. Which steady, hardworking seam bowler was a vital factor in Hampshire's 1961 county triumph?

10. Which enigmatic but prolific South African batsman joined the county in 1968?

11. Which Barbadian scored more than 19,000 runs for Hampshire between 1970 and 1987?

12. Who was captain when the county won the title for the second time in 1973?

13. Which West Indies bowler joined the club in 1979 and went on to take 824 wickets at an average of 18.64?

14. The county's lowest first-class score against them came in 1964 when they bowled out Yorkshire for 23. Which seamer did the damage with 6-10?

15. Which successful Hampshire keeper never played a Test but substituted for the injured Bruce French during the Test v New Zealand at Lord's in 1986?

16. Which long-serving Hampshire captain became a TV presenter and commentator after retiring in 1995?

17. Which Hampshire and England batting great retired in 2003?

18. Who did Hampshire defeat to win the 1988 Benson and Hedges Cup?

19. Which South African seamer took five wickets to claim the man of the match award?

20. What limited overs name did Hampshire drop in 2013?

KENT

1. When was the county club founded?

2. Kent have won the County Championship outright six times. In 1977 they shared the title with which other team?

3. What was the Spitfire Ground in Canterbury known as before its name change?

4. How many of their six Championship titles did Kent win before the First World War?

5. Which Golden Age bowling great, instrumental in Kent's title wins, was killed near Passchendaele in 1917?

6. Which Kent and England player scored more runs than anyone but Jack Hobbs, took more than 2000 first-class wickets, and held more than 1000 catches?

7. By what nickname was Kent and England leg-spinner Alfred Percy Freeman better known?

8. What amazing feat is Freeman the only player to achieve?

9. Who was captain when Kent won their fifth county title in 1970?

10. Which left-arm spinner was instrumental in that success?

11. In 1967 whose 54 in the final against Somerset helped Kent win their first Gillette Cup and won him man of the match?

12. In 1974 Kent defeated which side to win it again?

13. Who was captain in 1978 when the county won their last County Championship?

14. Which Pakistani international topped the county's batting averages that summer?

15. Which Barbadian played only five Tests for the West Indies but had 15 very successful seasons for Kent between 1966 and 1981?

16. What one-day trophy did Kent win in 2007?

17. Who scored Kent's highest individual score of 332 v Essex in 1934?

18. Which of Kent's great wicketkeepers, Alan Knott or Les Ames, holds the county's record number of dismissals in a season with 116?

19. Who was named Kent captain for the 2016 season?

20. What is the name of the Kent limited overs team?

LANCASHIRE

1. What flower is on the Lancashire badge?

2. When was the county founded?

3. How many times has the county won the County Championship, including their shared title?

4. In 1895 which batsman scored 424, still the highest score by an Englishman in first-class cricket?

5. Between 1926 and 1934, how many times did the county win the Championship?

6. Which player was captain for two of those triumphs, before leaving cricket to become a Tory MP and was killed in the Second World War?

7. With which left hander did Cyril Washbrook form a formidable opening partnership before the Second World War?

8. Which prolific all rounder twice achieved the double of 1000 runs and 100 wickets in a season during the 1930s but only played two Test matches for England?

9.   Lancashire shared the title with Surrey in 1950, a season which marked the emergence of which fast bowler?

10. Which trophy did Lancashire win three times between 1970 and 1972?

11. Who was the skipper who led them to those triumphs?

12. In the famous 1971 semi-final against Gloucestershire, which player hit 24 from an over in near darkness to win Lancashire the match?

13. Which spin bowler, who retired in 1989 aged 48, was known as Flat Jack?

14. Who was skipper in 1984 when Lancashire won the Benson and Hedges Cup?

15. Who did Lancashire hammer in the 1990 NatWest Trophy to secure a domestic Cup double?

16. Who was coach when Lancashire won their first outright county title since 1934?

17. Who was skipper?

18. Who is Lancashire's leading first-class run scorer with 34,222?

19. Who is their leading wicket-taker?

20. What are the limited overs team known as?

LEICESTERSHIRE

1. When was the club founded?

2. How many times have they won the County Championship?

3. Leicestershire play most of their matches at Grace Road. Which is the only other home ground they have used since 2000?

4. The father of Leicestershire's longest serving captain Charles de Trafford owned which cricket ground?

5. Which Leicestershire batsman passed 1000 runs every season between 1928 and 1950 and is his county's highest run scorer?

6. Which between-the-wars off-break bowler is the county's leading wicket taker and won nine Test caps for England?

7. Who was captain when Leicestershire won the County Championship for the first time in 1975?

8. Which batsman became the only man to ever play professional cricket and football on the same day in 1975 when he scored 51 not out for Leicestershire and then played for Doncaster Rovers in the evening?

9. Leicestershire's first taste of silverware had come under Illingworth in 1972 when they won the 1972 Benson and Hedges Cup. Who did they beat in the final?

10. Which Australian quick's three wickets were decisive in Leicestershire's victory?

11. Which seamer was man of the match when Leicestershire completed a memorable season by beating Middlesex in the Benson and Hedges Cup final of 1975?

12. What year did David Gower make his Leicestershire debut?

13. Which team did Leicestershire defeat in the 1985 final to add another Benson and Hedges Cup to their collection?

14. Which England player was man of the match after his match-winning, unbeaten 86?

15. Who was skipper when Leicestershire won their last County Championship title in 1998?

16. Which left-arm seamer who played for England had an important role in that Championship win?

17. Which South African batsman holds the record for the county's highest individual score, 309 not out v Glamorgan in 2006?

18. Who is current club captain?

19. How many times have Leicestershire won the T20 Cup in the last eight years?

20. What is the county's one-day name?

MIDDLESEX

1. When were Middlesex founded?

2. How many times have they won the County Championship title?

3. Which Scottish rugby union player captained Middlesex to their first county title in 1903?

4. Which noted Test player, administrator and author captained the county between 1908 and 1920?

5. Which great batsman was instrumental in the county's 1920 and 1921 title wins?

6. Name the batsman who scored a 1000 runs for Middlesex before the end of May in 1938, scoring every run at Lord's.

7. Middlesex won the 1947 title thanks to the run scoring of which dashing young batsman?

8. Which year did Denis Compton and Bill Edrich record their record 424 stand for the third wicket against Somerset?

9.   Which Middlesex player lost four toes in a boat accident while on tour for England in 1967–8 but still continued a successful career after?

10.   Who was appointed Middlesex captain in 1971, ushering in an era of success for the county?

11.   Which former Sussex and Somerset seamer topped the county's averages in the Championship-winning summer of 1976?

12.   In the 1980 side, which South African bowler took 85 wickets at 14.72?

13.   When did Mike Gatting take over the captaincy?

14.   Which West Indies quick who served the county between 1977 and 1988 was known by the nickname 'Black Diamond'?

15.   Which wicketkeeper holds the county's record for dismissals with 1223 over 23 seasons?

16.   Who is the only Middlesex bowler to have taken all ten wickets in an innings, in 1929 v Lancashire at Lord's?

17.   When did Middlesex win the last of their Championship titles?

18.   Which England spinner took 68 wickets in that season?

19. Who did Middlesex beat in a thrilling final by three runs to win the Twenty20 Cup in 2008?

20. What colour clothing do Middlesex wear in limited overs cricket?

NORTHAMPTONSHIRE

1. What year did the club join the County Championship?

2. How many times have they won the County Championship?

3. Before the First World War, which player did the 'all rounders double' of 1000 runs and 100 wickets four times?

4. Which burly Northamptonshire all rounder was voted one of *Wisden*'s five Cricketers of the Year in 1906?

5. By what name was fast bowler Edward Winchester Clark, who holds the record for taking the most wickets in the county's history and was capped by England in 1931, better known?

6. What ignominious record did Northants achieve between May 1935 and May 1939?

7. Where was Northamptonshire captain, England Test player and future selector Freddie Brown born?

8. Which fast-bowling great made his debut for the county in 1952 against the touring Indians?

9. Which successful Northants and England batsman retired suddenly aged only 29 at the end of the 1961 season?

10. Which tall, enigmatic fast bowler took 666 wickets at 19.53 apiece and played ten Tests for England before again retiring at 29?

11. Which silver-haired batsman who served the county for 18 years made a famous debut for England v Australia at Lord's in 1975, which earned him the BBC Sports Personality of the Year award?

12. By what nickname was hard-hitting Northants and England opener Colin Milburn universally known?

13. What did Northants win in 1976, their first ever trophy?

14. Who was man of the match after scoring a match-winning 65 to defeat Lancashire?

15. Which long-serving Northants seam bowler was nicknamed 'The Ghost'?

16. Which opening batsman was man of the match when the county defeated Leicestershire in the 1992 NatWest Trophy final?

17. Which Australian opener played for the county between 2001 and 2003 and scored the two highest individual scores in Northants's history?

18. Which all rounder sealed the county's T20 win in 2013 with a hat-trick?

19. Who is their current captain?

20. To what does the county's one-day name, the Steelbacks, refer?

NOTTINGHAMSHIRE

1. When was the county club founded?

2. How many times have they won the County Championship?

3. What is the name of their home ground?

4. Which batting great, who played all his 15 tests outside England, is the county's highest run scorer, and was instrumental in their 1907 title?

5. Name the captain who led the side to the title in 1929, during a 15-year stint in charge.

6. Two Notts fast bowlers were an integral part of the county's success between the wars, as well as forming part of Douglas Jardine's attack on the controversial 'Bodyline' tour. One was Harold Larwood. Name the other.

7. Which football-playing batsman's 312 not out against Middlesex in 1939 remains a club record?

8. The signing of which overseas player in 1968 is credited with halting the county's post-war decline?

9. Who led Notts to the title in 1981, their first for 52 years?

10. Name the seam bowler whose 105 wickets were pivotal in winning that title.

11. The county did the double in 1987, winning the title and which one-day trophy?

12. Who did they beat in the final?

13. In 1989 they won the Benson and Hedges Cup against Essex in a thrilling last-ball finish. Who hit the winnings runs?

14. Man of the match in that final was which prolific opening batsman and captain?

15. Which long-serving Notts keeper played 16 Tests for England but did not play more because his batting was not deemed good enough?

16. Who led Notts to their Championship win in 2005?

17. Nottinghamshire won the 2010 title on the last day of the season. On the back of whose century did they claim maximum batting points, which helped them pip Somerset?

18.   Which Kiwi bowler was pivotal in that campaign, finishing with 68 wickets, more than any other bowler?

19.   Who is the current county captain?

20.   What is the county's limited overs name?

SOMERSET

1. When was the county club founded?

2. How many times have Somerset won the County Championship?

3. Name the batsman who, during a 19-year career for the county before the First World War, was described by *The Times* as the 'most beautiful batsman of the time'.

4. Which hard-hitting batsman who played for the county between 1935 and 1954 scored the fastest century of the season on his debut, after missing the bus to get to the match and arriving late?

5. Which fast-bowling all rounder hit more than 500 sixes in his career between 1927 to 1950, accounting for a quarter of his runs?

6. What is the highest position finished in the Championship in the interwar years?
    a) 4th
    b) 5th
    c) 6th

7. The arrival of which former Yorkshire captain in 1971 saw an upturn in Somerset's fortunes?

8. Which fast bowler joined Viv Richards as overseas pro in 1977?

9. Who inherited the captaincy in 1977?

10. Somerset broke their trophy drought by winning the Gillette Cup and Sunday League in which year?

11. Which West Indies bowler took most wickets for Somerset in the Sunday League for six seasons between 1973 and 1982 and was also know for a distinctive underarm throw to the keeper?

12. Who did Somerset defeat to win the 1982 Benson and Hedges Cup, their second successive win in the tournament?

13. Who was man of the match in the 1983 Gillette Cup final with three wickets for 30?

14. Who led the side to that last trophy?

15. Which cricketer's diary of the 1983 season, *It Never Rains,* is considered by many to be one of the best cricket books written?

16. Which Australian batsman led Somerset to the 2001 Cheltenham and Gloucester Trophy?

17. Which South African opener holds the county's record for the most hundreds in a season, with 11 in 1991?

18. Which overseas batsman holds the county's record for the highest individual score with 342 against Surrey in 2006?

19. Who is the current county captain?

20. What limited overs name did the county recently drop?

SURREY

1. When was Surrey founded?

2. True or false. With 18 outright County Championship wins, Surrey are the game's most successful county.

3. Surrey won the first official County Championship title in what year?

4. The county won the Championship six times in the 1890s. Which great seam bowler was a major part in that success?

5. In 1899 whose 357, out of a record total of 811 against Somerset, still remains a club record?

6. Which batsman made his debut for Surrey in 1905?

7. The side was reliant on its batting during the barren years between the wars, but which fast bowler took 200 wickets in 1936 and 1937, a fine achievement given the batsman-friendly Oval pitch?

8. Surrey dominated post-war cricket, winning 10 titles in 12 seasons. Which captain won the Championship in all five years he was captain between 1952 and 1956?

9. The spin twins Lock and Laker were instrumental in that success, as was which tireless seam bowler?

10. Surrey's 1971 title came under the leadership of which skipper?

11. Who was the club's first overseas player in 1969?

12. Which left-arm seamer's short career was illuminated by a man of the match performance to give Surrey the 1982 NatWest Trophy?

13. Under whose captaincy did Surrey win a glut of trophies between 1998 and 2003, including three titles and two Benson and Hedges Cup victories?

14. Which hard-hitting batsman scored a record 268 in a one-day match v Glamorgan in 2002?

15. Which new competition did Surrey become winners of in 2003?

16. Who holds the record for the county's most appearances, with 598?

17. Who achieved the county's second highest first-class score when he scored 355 against Leicestershire at the Oval in 2015?

18. Who is the county's leading wicket taker with 1775?

19. Name the county's current captain.

20. At which ground do Surrey still annually play one first-class match and one one-day match each summer?

SUSSEX

1. When was the club founded?

2. How many times has it won the County Championship?

3. True or false. The first of those wins came in 2003.

4. Sussex's main ground is in Hove. Name one of its other two grounds that regularly host a first-class match each season.

5. Which Indian prince made his county debut for Sussex in 1895 and played with great success for the next 25 years?

6. Who did Sussex great John Langridge put on a first-wicket partnership of 490 runs with in 1933, the highest Sussex partnership and the fourth highest opening partnership of all time?

7. Which great Sussex and England bowler took 198 wickets in 1925 and a county record 2211 in a successful 25-year first-class career?

8. Which Sussex father and son played with great distinction for the county between 1924 and 1939, and 1949 and 1972?

9. Which post-war Sussex left-handed batsman stands equal third in the list of men with most first-class runs not to have played a Test and enjoyed a 22-year career for the county?

10. Which inaugural competition gave Sussex their first silverware in 1963?

11. Which England great led Sussex to that trophy?

12. Who was the batting hero with an undefeated 62 as Sussex chased down 207 against Somerset to win the 1978 Gillette Cup?

13. Who captained Sussex to second place in the Championship in 1981?

14. Which enterprising all rounder was man of the match for his heroics in the NatWest Trophy victory of 1986?

15. Who skippered Sussex to their first every Championship title in 2003?

16. Who was their coach?

17. Which Sussex bowler became the first to take a 100 wickets in a season since Andy Caddick and Courtney Walsh in 1998?

18. Which batsman hit a match-winning 335 not out to seal the title, the highest score in Sussex history until he bettered it himself in 2009?

19. Who is the current county captain?

20. What is the county's limited overs team called?

WARWICKSHIRE

1. When was the county formed?

2. How many County Championship titles have they won?

3. Other than Edgbaston, which is the only ground Warwickshire have used in the twentieth century for a first-class match?

4. Whose achievements before the outbreak of the First World War still rank him today as the county's greatest all rounder?

5. What was Warwickshire's surprise Championship success of 1911 attributed to?

6. Which leg spinner 'carried' the county's attack before and after the Second World War, helping win the 1951 County Championship, and is still the county's leading wicket taker?

7. Which belligerent England batsman's 66 won Warwickshire their first Gillette Cup against Worcestershire in 1966?

8. Who was the captain who led them to that trophy, during a stint of ten years in charge?

9. Strong batting was widely credited with winning them the 1972 County Championship. Who was their top run scorer that season and remains their highest run scorer to date?

10. Which hard-hitting batsman-wicketkeeper shared a county record 470 stand with West Indies ace Alvin Kallicharran against Lancashire at Southport in 1982?

11. The 1980s were a lean period until they won the 1989 NatWest Trophy against which side?

12. Which former Sussex all rounder was man of the match in that game and was the catalyst for the county's emergence as a force in the one-day game?

13. In what is widely regarded as the best domestic final in English cricket history, a ton by which Ugandan-born player allowed Warwickshire to chase down Sussex's 321 to win on the last ball of the game?

14. Which West Indies batsman reigned supreme in the summer of 1994 to help win Warwickshire the title?

15. Which seamer, who played twice for England, took 81 wickets that season to help clinch the title?

16. Who was captain for their 2004 title triumph?

17. In 2012, which former Surrey all rounder's form helped them clinch their latest county title?

18. In which year did the county win the T20 Blast?

19. Which New Zealand cricketer took most wickets in the competition with 25?

20. What is Warwickshire's T20 name?

WORCESTERSHIRE

1. What year did the club join the County Championship?

2. How many times has the county won the County Championship title?

3. What natural phenomena is the county's New Road ground prone to?

4. What name was jokingly given to the team in the first few years of the twentieth century because seven brothers from the same family played for the club?

5. Which long-serving player, captain and president kept the club alive financially during the lean years following the First World War?

6. Which professional bowler helped change the team's fortunes in the 1930s and still holds the county's best bowling figures of 9-23?

7. Who skippered the county to their first Championship title in 1964 and a successive title the following year?

8. Which stylish former Gloucestershire batsman scored his 100th first-class hundred in the 1964 season?

9. Name the seamer who formed a formidable and feared new-ball pair with fellow quick Len Coldwell during the 1960s.

10. Which prolific all rounder made his debut in the 1964 season?

11. Which New Zealand opener's runs were a vital part of Worcestershire 1974 county success?

12. Which all rounder made the switch to Worcestershire in 1987 and helped them seal titles in 1988 and 1989?

13. Which prolific batsman scored heavily during that period, including a county best 405 v Somerset at Taunton in 1988?

14. Who was skipper during this period?

15. Which seam bowler, who only played two Tests for England in 1939, is the county's leading wicket taker with 2143?

16. Which batting stalwart led Worcestershire to triumph in the 1994 NatWest Trophy final against Warwickshire?

17. Which Australian Test player was man of the match in that final for an unbeaten 88 and a miserly new-ball spell?

18. Who is the county's highest run scorer with almost 35,000 runs?

19. What trophy did Worcestershire win in 2007?

20. What is the current name of the Worcestershire T20 side?

YORKSHIRE

1. In what year was the county club founded?

2. What is the county's emblem?

3. How many outright County Championship titles have they won?

4. Which is the only outground where Yorkshire still play first-class cricket?

5. Who was captain for the county's first Championship in 1893?

6. Yorkshire won three successive titles between 1900 and 1902 thanks to contributions from their two great all rounders. Wilfred Rhodes was one – who was the other?

7. In 1908 Yorkshire bowled Northamptonshire out twice for the lowest aggregate total in first-class cricket history. The record still stands. What is it?

8. Which prolific opening batsman made his debut in the 1919 Championship-winning side?

9. How old was Wilfred Rhodes when he retired in 1930?

10. Who took over his mantle as the county's main left-arm spinner?

11. Which bowler took 200 wickets in his first full season for Yorkshire in 1951?

12. Who became Yorkshire's first professional captain of the modern era in 1960?

13. Who played a swashbuckling innings of 146 to give Yorkshire their first limited overs trophy when they defeated Surrey in the 1965 Gillette Cup final?

14. How many Championship titles did Yorkshire win in the 1960s?

15. Which successful captain was controversially sacked in 1970?

16. During a lean spell for the county, the 1987 Benson and Hedges Cup final victory in 1987 over Northants was a rare triumph. Who was man of the match with an unbeaten 75?

17. Who was skipper when the county won their first Championship title for 33 years in 2001?

18. Who is Yorkshire's all-time highest run scorer?

19. Who skipped Yorkshire to their 2014 and 2015 Championship triumphs?

20. What name do Yorkshire's one-day team play under?

MORNING SESSION

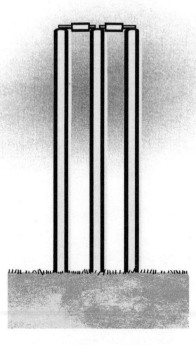

TMS GREATS – W.G. GRACE

1. In what year was Grace born?

2. Where was Grace born?

3. What do the initials W.G. stand for?

4. Two of Grace's brothers also played Test cricket for England. One was Edward. Name the other.

5. How old was Grace when he scored his first century, 170 for the South Wales Club against the Gentlemen of Sussex?

6. At which ground did Grace make a century against Australia on his debut for England in 1880?

7. What was Grace's highest Test score?

8. How many Test wickets did he claim?

9. In 1871 there were 17 first-class centuries scored in England. How many of them did Grace score?

10. Grace became the first batsman to achieve what feat in a match between the Gentlemen of the South and the Players of the South in 1873?

11. How many times did Grace complete the double of 1000 runs and 100 wickets in first-class cricket?

12. For whom did Grace play most of his county cricket?

13. What batting feat did Grace achieve in May of 1895?

14. What job did Grace qualify to be in November 1879?

15. Other than 'The Doctor' and later in his career 'The Old Man', what other nickname was Grace given?

16. How old was W.G. Grace when he played his last Test for England in 1899?

17. For how many seasons did Grace play first-class cricket?

18. In later life, Grace took up which sport, even founding its national association?

19. For which shortlived first-class team did Grace turn out until it folded in 1908?

20. In which year did Grace die?

THE EARLY YEARS

1. Who captained England's first overseas cricket tour in 1859?

2. Which exotic band of cricketers cerated great excitement among the British public when they toured England in 1868?

3. Who was the England captain who, before setting sail to Australia for the tour of 1882–3, promised that he would regain 'the Ashes'?

4. After England and Australia, which nation became the third to play Test cricket in 1889?

5. What name has been given to describe the era in between the formation of the official County Championship in the 1890 season to the outbreak of the First World War?

6. What nickname was given to Australian bowler Frederick Spofforth?

7. Name the cricketer who played for both Australia and England at Test cricket and whose legendary 'sixer' is said to have cleared the pavilion at Lord's.

8. Which later actor and Hollywood movie star led England's overseas tour of 1888–9?

9. By what name was Martin Bladen Hawke better known?

10. Which celebrated Aussie batsman and stylist was also a key figure in founding rugby league in his home country?

11. True or false. Cricket-loving author P.G. Wodehouse named his character Jeeves after the name of a Warwickshire cricketer.

12. Only two men have twice been made *Wisden* Cricketer of the Year. One was Jack Hobbs. Name the other.

13. Name South Africa's captain/wicketkeeper who led them to their first victory in tests against England at Johannesburg in 1906.

14. England Ashes-winning captain J.W.H.T. Douglas was an Olympic champion in which sport at the 1908 London games?

15. Legendary batsman C.B. Fry represented England at cricket and which other sport?

16. Fry also equalled the world record for which athletic event?

17. What did Australian captain Joe Darling fail to do in all five Tests of Australia's 1905 tour of England?

18. Name the American cricketer who headed the first-class bowling averages in 1908 with 87 wickets at 11.01, a feat that wasn't bettered until 1958.

19. At which South African ground did England play their last Test Match before the outbreak of the First World War in February–March 1914?

20. Which England bowler took a record 49 wickets in only four Test matches in the 1913–14 series v South Africa?

THE ASHES 1

1. In which newspaper was the obituary for English cricket printed after their defeat to Australia in 1882?

2. What is rumoured to be the contents of the small urn presented to the England captain after they regained 'the Ashes' in 1883?

3. The term 'the Ashes' went unused for 20 years until which victorious English captain wrote a book entitled *How We Recovered the Ashes*?

4. Which side held the Ashes at the outbreak of the First World War?

5. Who led the Australian side in their 5-0 whitewash of England in the 1920–1 series?

6. Which Australian spinner took 36 wickets in that series, including 9-121 at Melbourne?

7. True or false. England did not win a Test in 15 matches against Australia between the end of the First World War and 1925.

8. England regained the Ashes in 1926 with a 1–0 victory. The victory came in the last Test at which ground?

9. By what term was Bodyline less emotively known?

10. Harold Larwood played for which English county?

11. Which bowler famously removed Bradman for a golden duck in the second Test of the Bodyline series at Melbourne, his only Test wicket of the tour?

12. Name the Australian captain who reportedly told Plum Warner, the England manager: 'There are two teams out there. One is trying to play cricket, the other is not'?

13. Name the English fast bowler who refused to resort to captain Douglas Jardine's Bodyline tactics.

14. What was the result of the Bodyline series?

15. True or false. Harold Larwood never played another Test for England after that series.

16. How many wickets did Hedley Verity take in the second Test of the 1934 series at Lord's, which became known as 'Verity's Match'?

17. Who captained the Australians in the 1936–7 series when they came back form 2–0 down to win 3–2?

18. Which England batsman marked his Ashes debut with a century in the first Test at Trent Bridge in 1938?

19. The final Ashes Test at the Oval saw England's 903-7 and Hutton's 364 break Test records – both were eventually broken. But what other record still stands?

20. Which Ashes great was killed in action in Italy during the Second World War?

BETWEEN THE WARS

1. In what year was the first Test played after the end of the First World War?

2. How many of their 38 first-class matches did the touring 1921 Australians lose?

3. Frank Mann captained England in their five Test tour of South Africa in 1922–3. His son George captained England after the Second World War. Name the only other father and son to captain England.

4. South Africa's 30 v England in 1924 is the joint second lowest in Test history. It holds the record for what other ignominious achievement?

5. Which English bowler took 6-7 in the above innings?

6. Arthur Gilligan captained England on its tour of Australia in 1924–5. Which county did he play for?

7. Australian captain Herbie 'Horseshoe' Collins was well known for indulging in which pastime?

8. Which side toured England in 1928, playing their first ever Test matches?

9. Which famous West Indies cricketer was awarded a professional contract with Nelson in the Lancashire League in 1928 after his performances on their first Test tour of England?

10. Which West Indian batsman emerged as his nation's first great batting talent on the England tour in 1929–30 and later became the nation's first black captain?

11. Who captained New Zealand in their first ever Test match, against England in Christchurch in 1929?

12. What was the result of that inaugural four-match series?

13. Who won the inaugural series between South Africa and New Zealand in 1932?

14. Who captained England in the first Test against India in 1932?

15. Who led the Indian side in that Test match and went on to be named one of *Wisden*'s Five Cricketers of the Year?

16. In which city was the first Test on Indian soil played v England in December 1933?

17. Who scored 118 in that match, India's first Test century?

18. Against which nation did the West Indies secure their first series win in 1934–5?

19. The 'Timeless Test' between South Africa and England at Durban in 1939 had to be called a draw after eight days and two rest days for what reason?

20. Who contested the last Test before the outbreak of the Second World War?

TMS GREATS – DON BRADMAN

1. Name Don Bradman's birthplace.

2. What year was he born?

3. What was Bradman's middle name?

4. What equipment did Bradman famously use to hone his eye while playing solo cricket as a child?

5. What occupation did Bradman go into after leaving school?

6. Bradman scored a century on debut for New South Wales in the Sheffield Shield against which state side?

7. How many first-class matches had Bradman played before his Test debut against England at Brisbane in 1928?

8. How many runs did Bradman score in his first innings in Test cricket?

9. Recalled to the team for the third Test, Bradman hit his maiden Test century at which Australian ground?

10. He became known as 'The Don', but what was Bradman's nickname among his teammates in his early Test-match career?

11. Bradman scored his highest first-class score against Queensland at the SCG in 1930. What was it?

12. Bradman started his first tour of England in 1930 with 236 against which county?

13. In the third Test of that tour he scored 334, becoming the first player to score 300 in one day. At which English ground?

14. Name the English batsman who became Bradman's second and last Test match wicket at Sydney in 1933.

15. Which English bowler dismissed Bradman eight times, more than any other bowler?

16. Whose innings of 232 against England in the first Test of 1938 did Bradman rate as the best he'd ever seen?

17. With which other batsman did Bradman add 404 in 345 minutes to win the fourth Test at Leeds in 1948 with 15 minutes to spare?

18. Name the English bowler who dismissed Bradman for a duck in his final Test match.

19. What was Bradman's final Test average?

20. In what year did Donald Bradman die?

BOYCOTT'S BATSMEN 1

1. How old was Jack Hobbs when he scored his last first-class century in 1934?

2. In which Yorkshire town was Len Hutton born?

3. George Headley played league cricket in which county?

4. At which ground did Viv Richards score a then ODI record of 189 not out v England in 1984?

5. Name the bowler Gary Sobers hit for six sixes in one over for Nottinghamshire in 1968.

6. What is David Gower's middle name?

7. Graham Gooch became the 17th player in Test history to do what on his Test debut v Australia in 1975?

8. What was former Yorkshire and England captain Brian Close's first name?

9. Which English county did New Zealand opener Glenn Turner play for?

10.   Who took more Test catches, Steve Waugh or his brother Mark?

11.   How many Test matches did Allan Border play?

12.   Which former Yorkshire and England batsman went on to a 20-year career as a Test and first-class umpire?

13.   With which often overlooked batsman did Herbert Sutcliffe form a formidable opening partnership for Yorkshire for 15 seasons?

14.   With which batsman did Gordon Greenidge form a successful opening partnership for the West Indies, including 16 century stands?

15.   Which Indian batsman scored a record 34 Test-match centuries until it was broken by Sachin Tendulkar?

16.   Which Pakistani batsman is the only player apart from Geoff Boycott to score their hundredth first-class century in a Test match?

17.   Which Chappell brother had the highest Test batting average?

18.   Against which team did Alastair Cook score 294 in 2011?

19.   Joe Root was born in which Yorkshire city?

20.   How many Test match runs did Geoffrey Boycott score?

POST-WAR CRICKET

1. Which team toured England to contest the first Test series after the Second World War in 1946?

2. Which England bowler took 11 wickets on his debut in that series?

3. Post-war England poster boy Denis Compton was known by what nickname?

4. Compton also played football for which club side?

5. Lancashire all rounder Ken Cranston had an eventful eight-match Test career, including one as captain, before retiring in 1950 to take up a career as what?

6. How many matches did Bradman's Australian touring team lose on their 1948 tour of England?

7. Bradman topped the tour averages with 2428 runs at an average of 89.92. Which batsman was second with 1563 at 74.42?

8. New Zealand batsman Martin Donnelly played what sport for England?

9. Who captained the West Indies to their famous 3–1 series win in England in 1950?

10. Name the 'Three Ws' who excelled in that series for the West Indies and many after.

11. How was Leonard Hutton given out in his 100th Test innings v South Africa at the Oval in 1951?

12. India beat England for the first time a Test match in Madras in 1952. Which Indian bowler, whose name has entered cricket folklore for other reasons, took 12-108 in that match?

13. What was significant about Len Hutton's appointment as England captain in 1952?

14. Which England bowler was called for throwing on the 1953–4 tour of the West Indies?

15. Which 17-year-old batsman was at the crease for the West Indies when the above incident took place?

16. Which bowler bowled Pakistan to a series-levelling win in the final Test at the Oval on their first tour to England in 1954?

17. What nickname was given to English fast-bowling sensation Frank Tyson?

18. Russell Endean of South Africa became their first batsman in Test history to be given out in what manner against England at Cape Town in 1957?

19. Which two batsmen added 411 v West Indies at Edgbaston in 1957, still the highest partnership in England's history?

20. Who led England to a 5–0 rout of India in 1959?

AGGERS'S SEAMERS AND SWINGERS I

1. England bowler Les Taylor played for which county?

2. Which fast bowler was the quickset New Zealand cricketer to take 100 wickets in ODIs and took 87 Test wickets at 22.09?

3. Which bowler's 8-29 v Pakistan in 1977 are still the best Test-innings figures by a Windies paceman?

4. Who is the Burnley Express?

5. Name the Australian fast bowler who tried to use an aluminium bat.

6. Which English fast-bowling great only played two seasons of county cricket in a career spanning more than 40 years?

7. Curtly Ambrose was born on which Caribbean island?

8. Which Australian quickie dismissed Sachin Tendulkar the most times in his Test career?

9.   Shaun Pollock played for which English county in
      1996–2002?

10.   Which Australian fast bowler took 246 wickets in 60 Tests
      before retiring to play county cricket for Leicestershire?

11.   Which Pakistani paceman took 10 wickets in only his second
      Test against New Zealand in 1985?

12.   Which fast bowler took his 50th Test wicket in only his seventh
      Test in 2012?

13.   Which West Indian fast bowler broke Mike Gatting's nose
      in 1986?

14.   Which West Indian fast bowler broke Graham Gooch's hand
      in 1990?

15.   Which English fast bowler took 9-57 v South Africa in 1994?

16.   Which pace bowler became the fastest to take 400 Test wickets
      in July 2015?

17.   England Test bowler Bill Voce played for which county?

18.   True or false. West Indies fast-bowling pair Winston and
      Kenneth Benjamin are related.

19. Which quick became the first West Indian to take a hat-trick in Test cricket against Pakistan in 1959?

20. Which Indian pace bowler became the second after Kapil Dev to take 200 Test wickets?

TMS GREATS – FRED TRUEMAN

1. What was Fred Trueman's middle name?

2. What was Trueman's nickname?

3. What year did Trueman make his debut for Yorkshire?

4. In 1952 he made his Test debut against which nation?

5. Who was his opening partner who helped him reduce the opposition to 0-4 in the second innings of his debut?

6. At which Test ground did Trueman record his best Test figures of 8-31 in that same series?

7. Which football team did Trueman play for during his national service?

8. What nickname did West Indies fans give Trueman during the 1953–4 tour as a result of hostile bowling?

9. Which county colleague was Trueman's first England captain?

10. How many first-class hundreds did Trueman score?

11. With which other fast bowler did Trueman form a fruitful and lasting opening partnership for England?

12. At which ground did Trueman take most of his Test wickets?

13. In 1954 Trueman took his best first-class figures of 8-28 against which county?

14. In 1960 Trueman took more wickets in a first-class season than any other in his career. How many?

15. Who caught Neil Hawke to make Trueman the first bowler to take 300 Test wickets in 1964?

16. Against which nation in 1965 did Trueman play the last of his 67 Tests?

17. In 1972 Trueman came out of retirement to play six limited overs matches for which county?

18. Name the programme of pub sports Trueman presented for Yorkshire television between 1973 and 1978.

19. What year did Trueman make his debut as a *TMS* summarizer?

20. In what year did Trueman die, aged 75?

QUICK FIRE 3

1. Name the Australian term for extras.

2. Which county plays its matches at Grace Road?

3. Who was the first player to take a hat-trick for England in England in Tests?

4. Who was the last England bowler to take a hat-trick anywhere in Tests?

5. Which English bowler took a hat-trick against the West Indies in Barbados in 2004?

6. Former England captain Mike Atherton played for which county?

7. Who succeeded Clive Lloyd as West Indies captain?

8. Which umpire was famous for hopping around superstitiously when the score was on 111?

9. What is Marcus Trescothick's nickname?

10. What is Ian Botham's middle name?

11. Which folk singer's surname did Bob Willis add to his name by deed poll?

12. Where do Cambridge University play?

13. Which former English Test batsman won *Strictly Come Dancing* in 2006?

14. Which former English Test batsman didn't win it in 2012?

15. Name the Australian coach of Yorkshire.

16. Which England cricketer started out batting 11 but ended up opening the batting in a number of Test matches with success?

17. Name the domestic first-class tournament regional sides play for in India.

18. The Currie Cup is the first-class domestic tournament in which nation?

19. What year did the Indian Premier League start?

20. Who won the inaugural IPL?

NAME THE PLAYER 2

1. Horse (or 'Orse).

2. Chilly.

3. Pup.

4. Dazzler.

5. Yozzer.

6. Bacchus.

7. Gus.

8. K.P.

9. Arkle.

10. Sounda.

11. Lord Brocket.

12. Tubs.

NAME THE PLAYER 2

13.   Deadly.

14.   Watto.

15.   Virgil.

16.   Judge.

17.   Freddie.

18.   Pigeon.

19.   Punter.

20.   Afghan.

TUFFERS' TWIRLERS 1

1. Which bowler holds the record for most wickets taken by a spinner in a match?

2. Which left-arm spinner was the Chinaman named after?

3. Name the last underarm spinner to play Test cricket.

4. What's Shane Warne's middle name?

5. Which Yorkshire and England spinner recorded the amazing figures of 10-10?

6. Which county did Robert Croft play for?

7. Which Australian spinner became the first bowler to reach the milestone of 200 Test wickets?

8. Which successful West Indian spinner was such a poor batsman he never scored a half century in nearly 20 years of first-class cricket?

9. Which English spinner had a career that spanned five decades, between his debut in 1949 and his last match in 1982?

10. Indian spinner Bishan Bedi represented which English county for many years?

11. Which England spinner made his Test debut in 1968 but then didn't play again until eight years and 86 Test matches later?

12. Which English leg spinner played his only two Test matches in 2000 v Zimbabwe?

13. Name South Africa's most successful Test spinner.

14. Which successful Pakistani spinner played for Somerset in 1993–8?

15. Name the last spinner to take a Test hat-trick.

16. Which English left-arm spinner retired in 1988 aged 48 after taking 2068 first-class, the last man to break the 2000 mark?

17. Which international spinner went past Derek Underwood to become the most successful left-arm spinner in Test history?

18. John Emburey and Phil Edmonds played for which English county?

19. Which Yorkshire spinner of the 1970s and 1980s was known as 'Ferg'?

20. Which West Indian spinner, noted also for his fielding prowess, had a better bowling average than Lance Gibbs?

TMS GREATS –
GARY SOBERS

1. What is Gary Sobers's full name?

2. On which Caribbean island was he born?

3. How old was he when he made his Test debut in 1954?

4. Which West Indies spinner had fallen ill and so opened the way for Sobers's debut?

5. Against which team did Sobers achieve his highest Test score of 365 not out, then the highest Test score ever, in 1958?

6. True or false. That innings was Sobers's maiden Test hundred.

7. In which Welsh city did Sobers hit his six sixes off Malcolm Nash in 1968 – Cardiff or Swansea?

8. Against which team did Sobers achieve his best Test figures of 6-73 in 1968–9?

9. Sobers never took ten wickets in a Test match. True or false?

10. Sobers spent three seasons playing for which Australian state side?

11. What was Sobers's final Test batting average?

12. Which English county side did Sobers play for?

13. Name Sobers's cousin who played 24 Tests for the West Indies as a middle-order batsman and leg-spinner.

14. Which batsman said that Sobers's innings of 254 for the Rest of the World against Australia in Melbourne was the best he'd ever seen?

15. Sobers wrote a children's cricket novel called *Bonaventure and the Flashing Blade*. True or false.

16. In what year was Sobers knighted?

17. Sobers played his last Test in April 1974 against which touring side?

18. What was Sobers's last score in Test cricket: 20, 25 or 30?

19. Who succeeded Sobers as West Indies captain for the 1972–3 home series v Australia?

20. Which West Indies batsman did Sobers witness breaking his record for the highest score in Test cricket in Antigua in 1994?

ONE-TEST WONDERS

1. Scored a hundred for West Indies on debut in 1948 but never played again.

2. Scored 54 not out in his only innings for Australia v Sri Lanka at Perth in 1995 so doesn't have a Test batting average.

3. England opener who was struck on the head and retired hurt for 10 in 1984, making him the only Test opener never to have been dismissed.

4. Yorkshire seamer who took 1-65 v Australia at Trent Bridge in 1985, whose son also played for England.

5. New Zealander opener who scored 107 and 56 v Pakistan in 1973.

6. Yorkshire all rounder who scored a pair and didn't take a wicket against South Africa in 1999.

7. Played one Test for England v South Africa in 2008 without success, though his brother has played with rather more success for Australia.

8.   Brother of W.G. Grace who died of pneumonia two weeks after his Test debut.

9.   Essex all rounder who was called up to open the batting against Australia at the Oval in 1989.

10.   Glamorgan left-hander who opened against the Rest of the World at Lord's in 1970.

11.   Took 5-63 and scored 46 for Australia in the final Test of the 1977 Ashes for Australia.

12.   Spinner who bowled only eight overs for 53 runs for England in the final Test of the 2013 Ashes at the Oval.

13.   Played one Test for England in 1889 as captain but was more well known for a Hollywood acting career.

14.   Umpired 22 Tests and 23 ODIs from 1977 to 2001, but only played one Test for England in 1965 v South Africa.

15.   Surrey and Glamorgan opener, whose son was a more successful Test batsman, who played one Test v India in 1979 at the Oval.

16.   West Indian-born Surrey seamer who took four wickets in his first Test innings against South Africa in 1994 aged 33.

17. Portly Somerset spinner who scored four and failed to take a wicket in his only Test against India in 2006.

18. Danish-born, Kent and Sussex cricketer who played against the West Indies for England in the first Test in 2009, taking 1-122.

19. Aussie leg spinner who played aged 36 v South Africa in 2009 Cape Town, taking 0-149 in 18 overs.

20. Englishman who took 11-69 at an average of 8.72 v West Indies in 1933 aged 37, the only one-Test wonder to take more than seven wickets.

SAMSON'S STATS I

1. Who is the biggest run scorer in Test-match history with 15,921?

2. Who holds the record for the highest Test score of 400 not out?

3. Which two sides hold the record for the most consecutive series wins with nine?

4. What's the smallest margin of victory by runs in Test history?

5. Who holds the record for the most catches of a non wicketkeeper in Test history?

6. Who holds the record for the most sixes in a Test-match innings, hitting 12 in an innings of 257 not out for Pakistan v Zimbabwe in 1996?

7. Which English batsman holds the record for the most fours in a Test innings?

8. Which player holds the record for most ducks in a Test career?

9. Name the last English batsman to be dismissed by the first ball of a Test match.

10. Which West Indian part-time spinner has the worst bowling average of any bowler to take 100 Test wickets?

11. Herbert Sutcliffe of England and Everton Weekes of the West Indies share the record for taking the fewest innings to score 1000 Test runs. How many?

12. Who became the youngest person to score a Test match hundred when he scored 114 v Sri Lanka in 2001 aged 17 years and 61 days?

13. With 12, which batsman holds the record for most double centuries in Test cricket?

14. Which Australian wicketkeeper holds the record for the most stumpings in Test cricket with 52?

15. Which wicketkeeper did not concede a single bye against India in 2009 while they scored 726-9?

16. Which bowler/keeper combination has the most dismissals in Test history?

17. With 44,039, which bowler has bowled more deliveries in Test cricket than anyone else?

18. Who in 2004 became the youngest captain in Test history when he led his side against Sri Lanka aged 20 years and 358 days?

19. In 2013 which Australian bowler hit a record score of 98 not out to complete the highest ever Test innings by a number 11 batsman?

20. Which English bowler with 87 wickets holds the record for claiming the highest number of wickets in Test cricket without taking a single five-wicket haul?

THE ASHES 2

1. By what name did Bradman's touring Australians of 1948 come to be known?

2. Who succeeded Bradman as captain as Australia defeated England in 1950–1 4–1?

3. England retained the Ashes in 1953 for the first time in 19 years at which ground?

4. Who hit the winning runs?

5. Name the commentator who said at the time: 'Is is the Ashes? Yes! England have won the Ashes!'

6. Hutton was the victorious captain in Australia in 1954–5 thanks to which fast bowler who took 28 wickets in the series?

7. Which bowler took 46 wickets for England in the 1956 Ashes?

8. England retained the Ashes in that series by what scoreline?

9. Australia retained the Ashes down under 18 months later 4–0 under whose captaincy?

10. Which Australian fast bowler took 24 wickets at 19 apiece in that series?

11. Richie Benaud starred in the decisive fourth Test with a spell of 6-70 to clinch victory at which ground?

12. The final Test of the series marked the last Test of which England captain and batting great?

13. What was the score in the 1962–3 Ashes?

14. Which English batting great made his debut in the 1964 series?

15. Which Australian batsman, later a television commentator, scored 592 runs in the 1965–6 Ashes?

16. Which English bowler with 7-50 gave England a series-tying victory at the Oval in the rain-affected fifth Test?

17. Which fast bowler helped England win back the Ashes down under in 1970–1?

18. Who was England captain for that series?

19. What did England famously fail to get in the whole series?

20. How many Tests were there in that series?

TMS GREATS – SUNIL GAVASKAR

1. In which Indian city was Gavaskar born?

2. What score did Gavaskar make on his debut for Bombay in 1968?

3. Which team did he make his Test debut against in 1970–1, scoring 65 in his first Test innings?

4. In the fifth Test of that series Gavaskar scored 124 and 220 in the same match. Which Australian was the only other player to have scored a century and double century in the same Test?

5. True or false. Gavaskar's 774 runs at 154.80 is still the most runs scored in a debut series by any batsman.

6. With which English fast bowler did Gavaskar controversially 'collide' in the Test series in England in 1971?

7. At which English Test ground did Gavaskar score his first century against England in 1974?

8.   The final Test of the West Indies series in 1975 marked the start of a world record run of consecutive Test appearances. How many?

9.   In which country did Gavaskar score three consecutive centuries in 1977–8?

10.   Which team did Gavaskar's India defeat 1–0 in India in 1978–9?

11.   At which English ground did Gavaskar, with 221, and India nearly pull off a miraculous fourth innings chase of 438 in 1979, falling only 9 short?

12.   Whose record of 29 Test centuries did Gavaskar match when he scored a scintillating 121 off 94 balls against the West Indies in Delhi?

13.   Against which team did Gavaskar break the record, and in doing so scored his highest Test score of 236 not out?

14.   Who did Gavaskar replace for another stint as Indian captain in 1984–5?

15.   How many Test centuries did Gavaskar score?

16.   Who did India play in Gavaskar's last Test series in 1986–7?

17.   What record did Gavaskar achieve in the fourth Test?

18. What did he score in his final Test innings?
    a) 96
    b) 98
    c) 99

19. True or false. No player has scored more centuries against the West Indies than Gavaskar.

20. Which English county side did Gavaskar play for in 1980?

IN THE FIELD

1. What's the record for the most catches in a Test match by a non-wicketkeeper?

2. Which Pakistani batsman took four catches as a substitute fielder against Bangladesh in Multan in 2001?

3. Which England player took a diving one-handed slip catch to remove Adam Gilchrist in the 2005 Ashes at Trent Bridge?

4. Which English batsman holds the record for the most catches in a first-class career with 1018?

5. Who is second in that list with 876?

6. Which Australian batsman holds the record for being run out most times with 15?

7. Which Australian batsman holds the record for having run out most partners with 23?

8. Which player is credited with having effected the most run outs in Test history with 9?

9. Which player ran out three men in the 1975 World Cup final?

10. Who became the first fielder to take 150 catches in ODI cricket?

11. Who was first Test cricketer to take 100 catches in Tests?

12. Who has claimed most Test catches for England?

13. Which player has claimed most Test catches for a non-wicketkeeper for South Africa?

14. What is the record for the most amount of men out caught in the same Test match?

15. Three men have taken seven catches in a first-class innings. The most recent came in 2011 in a county match between Lancashire and Warwickshire. Who was the catcher?

16. Which South African batsman famously dropped Steve Waugh and was accused of 'dropping' the 1999 World Cup?

17. Which Australian dropped Kevin Pietersen in the 2005 Ashes at the Oval before he went on to score a series-winning century?

18. Name the Durham keeper who dropped Brian Lara when he was on 18. He went on to add a further 483 and score 501 not out.

19. The record for most batsmen to be run out in a Test innings is held jointly by India and Australia. What is it?

20. Which Indian player completed 184 Test innings without ever being run out?

TRUE OR FALSE

1. Gordon Greenidge's first name is Cedric?

2. England fast bowler Andy Caddick was born in New Zealand?

3. Alastair Cook was a talented choirboy in his youth.

4. Alec Stewart had football trials for Arsenal.

5. Nasser Hussain hit his last ball in Test cricket for four.

6. Test fast bowler Sajid Mahmood is a cousin of boxer Amir Khan.

7. Ian Bell's middle name is Ronald.

8. Kevin Pietersen started his county career at Hampshire.

9. Somerset seamer Colin Dredge was dubbed the Demon of Frome.

10. Merv Hughes took more Test wickets than Craig McDermott.

11. Saqlain Mushtaq pioneered the 'doosra'.

12.   Mark Butcher captained England for two Test matches in 1999?

13.   Mike Denness was born in Wales.

14.   New Zealand bowler Chris Martin has taken more Test wickets than he has scored runs.

15.   Dirk Nannes has played for both Australia and Zimbabwe in international cricket.

16.   Don Bradman hit six sixes in his entire Test career.

17.   Andrew Flintoff has commentated on snooker.

18.   England picked 27 different players in the 1989 Ashes series v Australia.

19.   Inzamam-ul-Haq once attacked a supporter who called him a fat potato.

20.   It is illegal to bowl underarm.

TMS GREATS – IMRAN KHAN

1. In what year was Imran born?

2. In which Pakistani city was he born?

3. In what year did Imran make his Test debut v England?

4. How many wickets did Imran take in that match?

5. How many years did he have to wait until he played his second Test?

6. Which England batsman was Imran's first wicket in Test cricket?

7. Name the Pakistani wicketkeeper who caught the catch to give him that wicket.

8. For which English county did Imran make his debut in the late summer of 1971?

9. For which side did Imran score his highest first-class score of 170 against Northamptonshire in 1964?

10. Imran established himself in the Pakistani side with 12 wickets against which side in 1977?

11. In a fast-bowling contest in Perth in 1978 Imran finished third in a strong field. Who finished ahead of him?

12. What county did Imran play for between 1983 and 1988?

13. Who did Imran succeed as Pakistani captain in 1982?

14. At which ground did Imran lead Pakistan to their first win on English soil for 28 years?

15. Against which side did Imran record his best Test figures of 8-58 at Lahore in 1981–2?

16. In what year did Imran lead Pakistan to their first series victory in England?

17. In 1990 Imran recorded his highest Test score of 136 against which country?

18. When did Imran play his last Test?

19. His last match as Pakistani skipper was which momentous, winning occasion?

20. What profession did Imran enter after his cricket career ended?

SWANNY'S ALL ROUNDERS

1. Who was the first Englishman to take 100 Test wickets and score 1000 runs?

2. Who is the last Englishman to have achieved it?

3. Who became the first Englishman to take five wickets and score a hundred in the same match in Barbados in 1974?

4. Which all rounder managed the same feat five times after that?

5. Which Bangladeshi all rounder was the last man to achieve this feat in a Test match in November 2014 v Zimbabwe?

6. Which Australian all rounder was the first to score a hundred and take ten wickets in a match against the West Indies in Brisbane in 1960?

7. Who became the first and only Pakistani cricketer to achieve that feat against India in Faisalabad in 1983?

8.   Which South African leggie became the first spinner to achieve the hundred and five wickets in a Test feat against England in January 1910?

9.   Who became the first player to complete the Test double of 200 wickets and 2000 Test runs in 1963?

10.   Which Englishman became the second after Ian Botham to achieve that feat?

11.   Of the eight players to have scored 3000 Test runs and taken 300 wickets, which of them has the highest batting average?

12.   Who has the best bowling average?

13.   Who is the only all rounder in history to have scored 5000 Test runs and taken 400 wickets?

14.   Who was the first cricketer to score 1000 runs, take 100 wickets and 50 catches in ODIs?

15.   Who in 1987 became the first player to score a hundred and take five wickets in an ODI?

16.   Which Englishman went one better, scoring a hundred and taking six wickets against Bangladesh in 2005?

17. Who became the first Englishman to open both the bowling and the batting in an ODI in 1986?

18. Which Pakistani has scored a half century and taken five wickets a record three times in his ODI career?

19. Which England player took a hat-trick and scored a half century against India at Trent Bridge in 2011?

20. Which Sri Lankan became the first man to score a fifty and take three wickets in an T20 international in 2006?

LUNCH

CRICKET QUOTES

1. Which English coach said after a drawn match: 'We flippin' murdered em!'

2. Which Australian cricketer said recently: 'He's [Steve Waugh] the most selfish cricketer I've ever played with.'

3. Which fast bowler said: 'I like to see blood on the pitch.'

4. Who described Graeme Hick as 'a flat-track bully'?

5. Which bowler told Brian Lara during his record-breaking innings of 375, 'I don't suppose I can call you a lucky bleeder on 347'?

6. Who said this: 'The other advantage England have got when Phil Tufnell is bowling is that he isn't fielding'?

7. Which Pakistani cricketer said: 'The next time I retire is the last time'?

8. Which TV commentator said: 'It's gone straight into the confectionery stall and out again'?

9. Which late American comedian described cricket as 'baseball on valium'?

10. Which England fast bowler said: 'A cricket tour in Australia would be a most delightful period in one's life if one was deaf'?

11. Who said: 'I'll tell you what pressure is. Pressure is a Messerschmitt up your arse. Playing cricket is not'?

12. Which Aussie said: 'Test cricket is bloody hard work, especially when you've got Sachin batting with what looks like a three metre wide bat'?

13. Who said this after retirement: 'The game of cricket existed long before I was born. It will be played centuries after my demise. During my career I was privileged to give the public my interpretation of its character in the same way that a pianist might interpret the works of Beethoven'?

14. Name the English spinner who said, 'The aim of English cricket is, in fact, mainly to beat Australia.'

15. Which batsman said 'I love England and I love cricket'?

16. Who said this: 'Part of the art of bowling spin is to make the batsman think something special is happening when it isn't'?

17. Who was Paul Collingwood paying tribute to when he said: 'Scored runs for funs, swung it both ways, could hit you in the head and had hands like buckets'?

18. Which England fast bowler told the opposition 'You guys are history' when he was hit by a bouncer and then went on to bowl them out?

19. Which England batsman said: 'The only thing I'm bloody frightened of is getting out'?

20. Which England fast bowler turned pundit once said: 'I am a born pessimist'?

LOOK IN THE BOOK I

1. From which book is this quote, 'What do they know of cricket who only cricket know?'

2. Which cricketer wrote an autobiography called *Don't Tell Kath*.

3. Which England captain's account of leading his side's tour of Australia was called *In Quest of the Ashes*.

4. Who wrote *The Art of Captaincy*?

5. Which England wicketkeeper wrote a book called *The Gloves Are Off*.

6. The wife of which England spin bowler wrote two accounts of being on tour with England in the 1980s?

7. Which Australian player wrote *Cricket Crisis*, an account of the Bodyline series?

8. Which prolific journalist wrote *Another Bloody Day in Paradise* about England's ill-fated tour of the West Indies in 1980–1?

9. Name the author of the award-winning account of life on the county circuit, *A Lot of Hard Yakka*.

10. Which former cricketer turned journalist and commentator wrote a book about his attempts to play baseball, titled *Playing Hard Ball*?

11. The title of Geoff Boycott's latest book was based on one of his favourite sayings. What is it called?

12. Whose most recent autobiography was called *Squeezing the Orange*?

13. Which stylish England batsman wrote a cricket crime novel called *Testkill*?

14. The biography of which West Indies great was called *Supercat*?

15. What was Michael Vaughan's autobiography called?

16. Which Australian captain's was called *At the Close of Play*?

17. What annual publication is known as 'cricket's Bible'?

18. Who is the current editor of that publication?

19. Which actor wrote a book about his lifelong love affair with cricket, named *Fatty Batter*?

20. Chris Waters wrote an award-winning biography of which England fast bowler?

I DON'T
LIKE CRICKET...

1. Who sang 'When an Old Cricketer Leaves the Crease'?

2. What was the name of the Terence Rattigan-scripted cricket film, made in 1953, and starring Jack Warner, Robert Morley, Denis Compton and Len Hutton?

3. Name the 1990s sitcom written about a cricket club, starring Robert Daws and Brenda Blethyn.

4. Who played Douglas Jardine in the Australia made-for-TV serial *Bodyline*?

5. Which Australian cricketer was the subject of a song by Paul Kelly?

6. Name the epic Indian drama about a small village that challenges their English colonial rulers to a game of cricket.

7. Which band with a cricket-related name have written two concept albums about the game?

8. Which songwriter wrote the theme for the World Cup in 1999, released the day after hosts England had been knocked out?

9. Name the 2010 documentary about the all-conquering West Indies side of the 1980s.

10. Which Australian mogul's attempt to revolutionize cricket was turned into a TV mini-series in 2012?

11. Which fictional character, created by George MacDonald Fraser, is alleged to have recorded the first hat-trick?

12. Name the 2008 novel by Joseph O'Neill about a Dutchman in New York who takes up cricket.

13. Which impressionist did a cricket spoof of Paul Hardcastle's '19' called 'N-N-Nineteen Not Out'?

14. Who performed the former BBC TV and now *TMS* theme tune 'Soul Limbo'?

15. Which band sang in 'Dreadlock Holiday', 'I don't like cricket...I love it?'

16. Who sang 'Mambo No. 5', which was used as the theme tune for Channel 4's coverage of cricket between 1999 and 2005?

17. Which Australian band had a top-five hit in the UK in 1976 with 'Howzat'?

18. Which former English batsman wrote a song in memory of Ben Hollioake?

19. Which Australian fast bowler released a single called 'You're the One for Me' featuring acclaimed Indian singer Asha Bhosle?

20. Which English fast bowler appeared in an episode of *Dad's Army*?

TMS QUOTES

Name the commentator or summarizer:

1. 'The total, Hutton's total, 332. It sounds like the total of the whole side. The England total 707 for 5, and the gasometer sinking lower and lower.'

2. (On Inzamam Ul-Haq being out hit wicket) 'Like an elephant trying to do the pole vault.'

3. 'I can see a butterfly walking across the pitch, and what's more it appears to have a limp.'

4. 'What a dipstick. To get a start like that and spoon it almost. That was like my mum hanging out the washing.'

5. 'The other hazard at the moment is a colony of silver gulls, several hundreds of them. At first they pitched on the top of the stand as if they were vultures recruited for Lillee...'

6. 'And he's bowled him! Cleaners! Middle stump absolutely knocked out.'

7. 'He's been feng shui'd... He's had his furniture rearranged.'

8. 'Cunis . . . a funny sort of a name . . . neither one thing nor the other.'

9. (After a block of cheese was thrown on the pitch at Headingley) 'We'll have to get CSI Yorkshire to dust the cheese for prints.'

10. 'Fielders scattering like missionaries to far places.'

11. 'Goodbye from Southampton. Now over to Edgbaston for some more balls from Rex Alston.'

12. 'This time Vettori lets it go outside off stump, good length, inviting him to fish, but Vettori stays on the bank and keeps his rod down . . .'

13. 'I think I might know a little bit about fast bowling.'

14. 'Australia all out for 348 on a golden evening at the Oval.'

15. 'That was a marvellous innings from Allan Lamb. Certainly worthy of a bottle of Bollinger – if he can find one in Kingston tonight.'

16. (On a bowler's distinctive action) 'He reminds of Groucho Marx chasing a pretty waitress.'

17. 'Warne in to bowl and Pietersen swings into this and *mows* the ball away.'

18. 'Goddard running in with his stump, being chased harum-scarum by lots of West Indian supporters. Such a sight never been seen before at Lord's.'

19. 'Oh look, another claret-coloured bus. I love these claret-coloured buses. They give me all sorts of ideas...'

20. '[Strauss] sticks out his left hand – he is left-handed so that is a minor help I suppose – and glory be! It stuck.'

GOOGLIES

1. Who invented the googly?

2. Which county do Mustard and Onions play for?

3. What was Michael Angelow famous for?

4. The names of which two English players were written on the side of a pig which ran on the ground of the 1982 Ashes Test in Brisbane?

5. What did Ian Botham joke that Mike Gatting thought he was catching when tumbled to catch Dennis Lillee in the 1981 Headingley Test?

6. Which Pakistani cricketer once bowled four deliveries with one hand, and two with the other at Taunton in 1954?

7. How did Derbyshire bowler John Kelly record the figures of 0.0 overs, 0 maidens, 4 runs and 0 wickets in 1955?

8. With what part of his clothing did Sri Lankan Russel Arnold catch English batsman Marcus Trescothick at short leg in 2001?

9. Which Sussex bowler holds the record for most consecutive scoreless innings with 12, 'achieved' in 1990?

10. Who was the eldest Test debutant, aged 49 and 119 days old?

11. Who became the oldest ever Test player when he played his last Test v West Indies in 1930, aged 52 and 165 days?

12. Which English left-handed batsman averaged 59.23, the fifth highest in Test history, but only played 20 Tests due to selectorial fickleness?

13. Which Aussie became the first batsman to wear a helmet in a Test match?

14. What feat did Geoff Boycott achieve in his comeback Test in 1977 against Australia at Trent Bridge?

15. For what rather sad fact is English one-cap wonder Jack MacBryan better known?

16. Which South African and then Zimbabwean player holds the record for the longest gap between Test appearances of 22 years?

17. Which English bowler was picked in 2003 after last playing in 1993, a hiatus of 115 matches, the longest in history?

18. Bernard Tancred holds the record for the lowest score of a batsman carrying his bat in Tests, for South Africa v England in 1889 in Cape Town. The team total was 47 – what was his score?

19. Which Zimbabwean batsman became the first player to carry his bat through an ODI innings against England at Sydney in 1994?

20. Which Nottinghamshire bowler became the only player in English first-class history to be timed out in a match against Durham University in 2003?

MEN IN WHITE COATS

1. Which umpire has written one of the biggest selling sporting biographies in British publishing history?

2. Which umpire holds the record for officiating in most Tests?

3. Who holds the record for umpiring the most Tests by an English umpire?

4. Name the Australian who umpired the first two Test matches ever played in 1877.

5. Which country is umpire Russell Tiffin from?

6. Which Daryl or Darrell officiated in most Tests – Harper or Hair?

7. Which long-serving English umpire was described by Don Bradman as the greatest he played under?

8. Which former England all rounder stood in 25 Tests as an umpire?

9. Name South Africa's longest serving umpire.

10. Which English umpire created a sensation when he refused to take the field in 1973 after the West Indies team disputed one of his decisions?

11. Which Australian umpire controversially no-balled Muttiah Muralitharan seven times in three overs in 1995?

12. Which umpire is famous for his 'crooked finger of doom'?

13. Which Australian umpire made his first-class debut as an official aged 24, his ODI debut aged 27 and his Test debut just a year later in 2000?

14. Which current umpire won the ICC Umpire of the Year in three consecutive years, 2009, 2010 and 2011?

15. Which serving English umpire played 18 ODIs for England as a wicketkeeper?

16. Which former umpire has the nickname 'Slow Death'?

17. Which famous English umpire ended the career of South African bowler Geoff Griffin when he called him for throwing in an exhibition match between England and South Africa at Lord's?

18. Which English umpire played one Test as an opening batsman against India in 1986?

19. Which English umpire is the only official to ever score a goal against Manchester United and stand in a Test match?

20. Name the Australian umpire who fell out with Ray Illingworth's England side during the acrimonious 1970–1 Ashes series down under.

FAMILY TIES

1. Name the Test-playing grandfather of Ian, Greg and Trevor Chappell.

2. What was Alec Bedser's twin brother called?

3. What relation is current England Test batsman Nick Compton to batting great Denis Compton?

4. Name the younger brother of Australian Test batsman Mike Hussey.

5. Former skipper Tony Greig's brother played two tests for England in 1982. What was his name?

6. What is the name of the father of England Test bowler Simon Jones, who also played Test cricket for England?

7. What happened to Robin Smith's brother Chris on his Test debut against New Zealand in 1983?

8. Yograj Singh played one Test for India v New Zealand in 1981. Name his son.

9. Doug Bracewell is the son of which New Zealand Test bowler – Brendan or John?

10. Which famous Test-playing Mohammad is father of current Pakistani player Shoaib – Hanif or Mushtaq?

11. What relation are Brian Lara and Dwayne Bravo?

12. Which Test side boasted three pairs of brothers in its side against New Zealand in 1997?

13. Who were the first pair of twins to represent their country?

14. Shaun Marsh and Mitchell Marsh are the sons of which Aussie Test player?

15. The grandson of which West Indian batting great played 15 Tests as a seam bowler for England?

16. Name the son of Sir Len Hutton who played five Tests for England.

17. Which country boasts the most amount of brothers from the same family to play Test cricket?

18. Name the only brothers who have played Test cricket AGAINST each other.

19. The niece of which Aussie great is the current Australian women's wicketkeeper?

20. How many members of the Cowdrey family have played first-class cricket?

CRICKET TERMS I

Give the terms for the following:

1. Two ducks in each innings.

2. Out first ball.

3. A ball that doesn't bounce.

4. A ball short of a length, begging to be hit.

5. An opener who bats through is not out when the rest of his team is dismissed.

6. A full ball intended to go under a batsman's bat.

7. A fruity term for a new ball.

8. Hitting the ball on to one's own stumps.

9. Unluckily caught via a fine edge down the legside.

10. Running out the non striker when he ventures from his crease.

11.   The area of the field between deep mid-wicket and wide long on, where many a slog goes.

12.   The sound the stumps make when broken, which every batsman dreads to hear.

13.   A medium-paced bowler.

14.   An unintentional inside edge down to the fine leg, passing in front rather than behind the batsman's pads.

15.   A pitch taking much spin. A turner.

16.   A very easy catch.

17.   The finger spin equivalent of the googly.

18.   Hanging one's bat limply outside off stump.

19.   A wet pitch, difficult to bat on.

20.   The score of 111.

ANAGRAMS

1. The Kit Moaner.

2. Brat Sad Tour.

3. Pekinese Invert.

4. Weave Thugs.

5. Band Random.

6. Manager News.

7. Helpful Lint.

8. Vulgarians Ask.

9. A Major Style.

10. Panache Pill.

11. Encoded Girl.

12. Brandy Store.

13. Orally Writhing.

14. Germany Vote.

15. Coldly Evil.

16. Bottle Turn.

17. Disable Liver.

18. Fearful Pile.

19. Hoard Grunge.

20. Alcohol Punks.

INITIAL IMPRESSIONS

What do the following acronyms or initials mean?

1. MCG

2. WACA

3. LBW

4. MCC

5. IPL

6. DRS

7. ECB

8. ODI

9. SLA

10. CMJ

Name the surname of these players from their initials:

11. WPUJC

12. IT

13. DI

14. IVA

15. VVS

16. RGD

17. DCS

18. LRPL

19. FMM

20. SCJ

BEST OF BEARDERS 2

1. Which Welshman who scored more than 36,000 first-class runs had his sole Test cap taken away when England's matches against the Rest of the World in 1970 were ruled as not counting as Test matches?

2. The highest Test innings without an extra is what?
   a) 308
   b) 328
   c) 348

3. What is the most amount of wickets to fall on any day of Test cricket?
   a) 23
   b) 25
   c) 27

4. The 1948 touring Australians hold the record for scoring the most runs in a day of first-class cricket, v Essex. What did they score?
   a) 721
   b) 731
   c) 741

5.   Which Zimbabwean bowler who ended his career in 2000 has the lowest batting average (2.00) of any player to have had more than 20 innings?

6.   What record does the Ashes Test between England and Australian in Melbourne in December 1982 hold?

7.   What are the most wickets to have fallen in a Test match without the batting side having a run on the board?

8.   How many ducks did Don Bradman make in his Test career?
        a) 5
        b) 7
        c) 9

9.   Which English bowler was responsible for two of those ducks?

10.   Which English batsman is the only player to score a triple century in first-class cricket in three different decades?

11.   What is the lowest score in first-class cricket of any batsman who has carried their bat through an innings?
        a) 5
        b) 7
        c) 10

12.   Who was the last England batsman to carry his bat in Test cricket, for 228 v New Zealand in 1997?

13. Who has the record for most runs without a half century in Test cricket?

14. Who holds the record for longest run of consecutive innings without a duck with 119 between 1982 and 1990?

15. Which cricketer scored 341 runs in a Test against South Africa in 2003 yet still ended up on the losing side?

16. Which former England opener scored a hundred in each innings of a county match with a runner for Lancashire in 1982?

17. Which New Zealand tailender was responsible for the longest duck in Test history v South Africa in 1998–9, taking 77 balls and 101 minutes?

18. Who is the only English batsman to average more than 100 in successive first-class seasons?

19. What is the lowest first innings score in Test history which has seen a side win by an innings?
    a) 132
    b) 152
    c) 172

20. What is the lowest total a side has defended in the fourth innings of a Test match?
    a) 75
    b) 85
    c) 95

THE PRESS BOX

1. From whom did Aggers inherit the job of BBC cricket correspondent?

2. Who is the current *Times* cricket correspondent?

3. Who was the *Daily Telegraph* cricket correspondent in 1946–75?

4. For which newspaper is Mike Selvey currently cricket correspondent?

5. Which former England bowler was Richie Benaud's commentary partner on the BBC for much of the 1970s and 1980s?

6. What match was Benaud's last commentary on UK television?

7. Which Australian commentator was known for his love of pigeons?

8. Which commentator was fond of calling a broadcast a 'telecast'?

9. Who was the BBC's first cricket correspondent?

10. Which former England player wrote for the *Independent* and then *Daily Telegraph* after his retirement in 1993?

11. Who edited *Wisden* for two stints between 1993 and 2000 and 2004 and 2007?

12. Geoff Boycott has a column for which newspaper?

13. Which respected Australian cricket writer has written books about Shane Warne, Jack Iverson and Warwick Armstrong?

14. Name the current cricket correspondent of the *Sun*.

15. Which revered *Times* cricket writer is believed to have attended more than 400 Test matches?

16. Which West Indies commentator and writer covered cricket from 1958 until shortly before his death in 2016?

17. Richie Benaud took up a journalism position doing the police rounds for which British weekly newspaper?

18. Which famous, oft-quoted cricket correspondent was also a music critic?

19. Which acclaimed Scottish-born cricketer, writer and journalist was known as 'Crusoe'?

20. When England were one short on the evening before the 1963–4 Bombay Test which then correspondent was put on standby to play?

AFTERNOON
SESSION

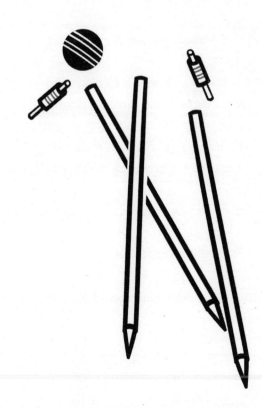

TMS GREATS – IAN BOTHAM

1. Where was Ian Botham born?

2. In which town did he go to school?

3. What year did he make his debut for Somerset?

4. Who hit him in the mouth with a bouncer that year, forcing him to spit out some teeth but carry on batting?

5. For which football team did Botham make 11 appearances in the Football League as a centre back between 1980 and 1985?

6. Against which side Botham make his Test debut in 1977?

7. How many wickets did he take in the first innings?

8. Against which team did Botham record his best Test bowling figures in 1978?

9. On 30 August 1979, in his 21st Test, Botham reached what landmark?

10. What make of bat did Botham use for most of his career?

11. What was highest Test score?

12. What was Botham's specialist fielding position?

13. Against which side did Botham fail to score a Test century?

14. How many Tests was Botham captain for in 1980 and 1981?

15. Which New Zealand batsman did Botham remove with his first ball back in Test cricket in 1986 following a drugs ban?

16. Against which team did he score his final century for England in 1986?

17. In what year did Botham complete his first charity walk, John o'Groats to Land's End?

18. Against which side did Botham play both his last Test and ODI in 1992?

19. In what year did Botham retire?

20. Botham's son Liam played first-class cricket for which county?

BOYCOTT'S BATSMEN 2

1. What happened to David Gower's first ball in Test cricket?

2. Which English batsmen made a century in his debut Test against Australia in 1993?

3. Which left-hander, called into replace a certain Yorkshire opener for England in 1973, scored 214 not out v India in his third Test at Edgbaston?

4. Which Australian opener holds the highest Test score by an opener?

5. Which county did Virender Sehwag play for in 2003?

6. Chris Gayle smashed a triple century for the West Indies in 2010 against which country?

7. Wally Hammond played his cricket for which English county?

8. Which Australian great scored 311 against England at Old Trafford in 1964?

9.   Other than Graham Gooch, Len Hutton and Wally Hammond, who's the other Englishman to score a Test triple century?

10.   Name the Australian batsman who scored an unbeaten 269 for Australia against the West Indies in Hobart in December 2015.

11.   Which South African opener scored 277, 85 and 259 in consecutive innings against England in 2003?

12.   Which Pakistani batsman holds the record for the slowest Test hundred, taking 557 minutes to score it against England in Lahore in the 1977–8 series?

13.   Who holds the record for the slowest hundred scored by an Englishman in Test cricket?

14.   Which England opener's 262 not out helped save England from defeat in Kingston in 1974?

15.   Name the first England batsman to make hundreds on all six traditional Test grounds: Old Trafford, Edgbaston, Headingley, Lord's, Trent Bridge and the Oval.

16.   Which Australian batsman averaged 57.28 in Tests at home, but only 25.68 in England?

17.   Who averaged 101.70 in first-class cricket in England in 1990?

18. Which touring batsman scored 1000 runs before the end of May in 1973?

19. Name the batsman who scored 108 in his first Test innings in 1970–1 and then 182 in his final innings, in 1983–4.

20. Which batsman twice averaged more than 100 in a first-class season, in 1971 and 1979?

ASHES 1970s

1. Which Australian bowled his side to victory at Lord's on his Test debut in the second Test of the 1972 series with 16 wickets?

2. Which England spinner took ten wickets at Headingley in the fourth Test to put England 2–1 up?

3. Which batsman's fourth innings 79 was instrumental in sealing a five-wicket win for Australia in the last Test to level the series 2–2?

4. Which England all rounder made his debut in the first Test of that series?

5. Australia 'brutally and unceremoniously' won the Ashes back in 1974–5 thanks to which fast-bowling pair?

6. Who was the defeated England captain?

7. Which Australian batsman became the first player to score an Ashes century in a single session since Don Bradman?

8. Who was flown out to help the battered England team aged 41 and played in the second Test at Perth without any match practice?

9. Which 37-year-old left-handed opener topped England's Test averages with 43.33?

10. In the 1975 Ashes, who replaced Denness as England captain after England lost the first Test at Edgbaston?

11. What prevented England or Australia winning the delicately poised third Test at Headingley?

12. Australia won the 1977 Centenary Test by the same margin they won the first Test in 1877. What was it?

13. Which English batsman scored a Test-career best 174 to almost snatch a win for England?

14. By what score did England regain the Ashes in the 1977 series?

15. Which England all rounder made his debut in that series?

16. Who was the victorious England captain?

17. Who was at the non-striker's end when Geoff Boycott drove Greg Chappell for four to record his 100th first-class century in the fourth Test at Headingley?

18. England retained the Ashes 5–1 in 1978–9 against a depleted Australian side. But which bowler took 41 wickets at 12.85 in that series for the home side?

19. Who was Australia's defeated captain?

20. Name the Australian opener who collapsed on the pitch after being hit in the chest by Bob Willis.

TMS GREATS – VIV RICHARDS

1. On which Caribbean island was Richards born?

2. What year did Richards arrive in England seeking to improve his cricket?

3. Which two other players did Richards share a flat with when he was taken on by Somerset in 1974?

4. Who was Richards's first captain at Somerset?

5. Against which team did Richards make his Test debut in 1974?

6. He scored his maiden Test century in that series. What was his score?

7. In the 1975 World Cup final, Richards ran out both Chappell brothers and which other Australian?

8. In a remarkable 1976, how many Test centuries did Richards score in the 11 Tests he played?

9. His highest career score came during that year, 291 at which English Test ground?

10. In 1979 Somerset won the Gillette Cup, their first silverware. Richards scored 117 in the final against which county?

11. In 1981, Richards scored another one-day century to win Somerset the Benson and Hedges Cup. Who were their unlucky opponents that day?

12. What year was Richards made West Indies captain?

13. Which overseas player did Somerset seek to replace Richards with at the end of the 1986 season, causing a bitter feud?

14. Which Lancashire league club did Richards play for in 1987?

15. Richards scored the then fastest century in Test cricket history in the fifth Test against England in Antigua in 1986. How many deliveries did it take him?

16. Against which team did Richards have least Test success, averaging 41.96 against them, compared to a career average of 50.23?

17. In seven years as West Indies captain, how many Test series did Richards lose?

18. In 1990, Richards returned to county cricket for which team?

19. Richards's last Test in 1991 was played against which side?

20. Which American professional boxer was Richards often compared to in looks and build?

ASHES 1980s

1. Which team won the 1982–3 Ashes down under?

2. Who was England captain for that series?

3. Who caught Jeff Thomson at slip via Chris Tavaré to win the fourth Test for England by 3 runs?

4. Which English nightwatchman narrowly missed out on a century in the final Test at Sydney?

5. Which Australian batsman earned the nickname 'The Happy Hooker' for the number of times he was caught hooking in the 1985 series?

6. Which England opener's 175 in the first innings of the first Test at Headingley set up England's victory?

7. Who was the victorious England skipper?

8. At Edgbaston in the decisive fifth Test, Ian Botham hit his first ball for six. Who was bowling?

9. Which Australian batsman was controversially caught close in off Phil Edmonds's bowling after the ball ricocheted from Allan Lamb's leg?

10. Whose 10 wickets earned him man of the match in that match?

11. Which English batsman topped the 1985 series batting averages with 527 runs at 87.73?

12. Which English cricket correspondent famously said this about the 1986–7 Ashes squad: 'There are only three things wrong with the English team – they can't bat, they can't bowl, and they can't field'?

13. Which England batsman scored hundreds in three consecutive Tests in that series?

14. Which English wicketkeeper scored a maiden Test century in the second Test at Perth?

15. Which English batsman made his only Test appearance in the fourth Test, scoring 11?

16. Which surprise Australian debutant was man of the match in their fifth Test consolation victory?

17. By what score did Allan Border's Australians beat England in the 1989 Ashes?

18. England famously used 29 players in that series. How many did Australia use?

19. How many runs had Steve Waugh amassed before he was dismissed for the first time in the series in the first innings of the third Test?

20. Which fast bowler made his Test debut for England in the fifth Test at Trent Bridge?

ASHES 1981

1. By what has the 1981 Ashes become more popularly known?

2. Who was captain of the Australian touring side?

3. Which seam bowler made his debut for Australia in the first Test at Trent Bridge?

4. What happened for the first time in England in that first Test which has since become commonplace?

5. Name the England batsman who bagged a pair in England's defeat in the first Test.

6. Which England player emulated that feat in the draw at Lord's?

7. Which keeper was dropped after the first Test to make way for Bob Taylor?

8. Who was the chairman of selectors who accepted Botham's resignation as captain?

9. Who scored a first innings century for Australia in the third Test at Headingley?

10. Graham Dilley is rightly praised for his role in a 117-run second innings partnership with Botham. But whose contribution to a 67-run ninth wicket partnership was also vital?

11. What were Australia dismissed for in their second innings as England won by 18 runs?

12. True or false. England became the first side to win a Test match after following on?

13. What was unusual about the fourth Test at Edgbaston?

14. What were Botham's figures in a spell of 28 balls to win the match?

15. Where was the fifth Test held?

16. Who was batting at the other end while Botham scored a blazing 118 in England's second innings?

17. Which Australian fast bowler was called up from playing league cricket near Blackpool and made his debut at Old Trafford?

18. Which Australian scored an unbeaten 123 as his side slid to a match and series defeat?

19. Which England player dropped Aussie debutant Dirk Wellham on 99 in the last Test at the Oval to give him the chance to complete a century?

20. Which England player made his one and only Test appearance in that match, scoring 0 and 13?

ASHES 1990s

1. Which England player had to stand in as captain for the injured Graham Gooch in the first Test in the 1990–1 series?

2. Whose spell of 6-47 in the second innings of that match proved decisive in winning the match for Australia?

3. Which England batsman made his maiden Ashes century in the third Test at Sydney?

4. Which Australian scored a hundred on his debut in the fourth Test?

5. Who succeeded Graham Gooch as captain when he resigned the captaincy once Australia had claimed the series?

6. Who was England coach for this series?

7. Who was named Australia's man of the series?

8. Which Somerset opener played the only two Tests of his career for England in the 1993 series?

9. Which Australian batsman laid down a marker for the 1994–5 series by hitting the first ball of the first Test for four?

10. Who was Australian captain for this series?

11. Which Australian fast bowler was named man of the series?

12. Who took most wickets for England with 20?

13. Who scored a double century to help give England victory in the first Test of the 1997 series at Edgbaston?

14. Who scored a century in each innings at Old Trafford in the third Test of that series to help pull Australia level?

15. Which England bowler made his only appearance in the fourth Test at Headingley, failed to take a wicket, and never played for England again?

16. Who took 11 wickets in the final Test in 1997 at The Oval to give England a consolation victory?

17. What was the score in the 1998–9 Ashes series?

18. Who captained England?

19. Whose second innings 6-60 helped win victory for England in the fourth Test at Melbourne?

20. Who was Australia's highest wicket taker in that series with 27?

TMS GREATS – LILLEE AND THOMSON

1. Which state was Lillee born in?

2. Which side did he make his Test debut against at Adelaide in 1970–1?

3. Who was his first Test wicket?

4. What year was Lillee named as one of *Wisden*'s Five Cricketers of the Year?

5. Which series did Lillee return from his first back injury to play in?

6. Complete the rhyme coined during that series as Lillee and Thomson ripped England to shreds: 'Ashes to Ashes, dust to dust...'

7. Which Australian bowler's record of 248 wickets did Lillee break in 1981?

8. With which Pakistani batsman did Lillee have an onfield altercation in 1981?

9. How many catches did Rod Marsh take off Dennis Lillee's bowling in Tests?
    a) 85
    b) 95
    c) 105

10. Which county did Lillee play for in 1988?

11. In which state was Jeff Thomson born?

12. Which West Indies batsman rated Thomson as the fastest he ever faced?

13. How many wickets did Thomson take on Test debut against Pakistan in 1972/73?

14. During the 1974–5 destruction of England, which batsman did one of Thomson's deliveries strike in a delicate area, forcing him to retire hurt?

15. At which Australian ground in that series did Thomson take his best Test figures of 6-46?

16. Which teammate did Thomson collide with on the field in 1976, breaking his collarbone and, some believe, reducing his pace forever?

17. When he wasn't selected for the 1981 Ashes, which county team did he play for?

18. Who did Thomson replace in the Australian team for the second Test against England in 1982–3?

19. In his last Test match, at the Oval against England in 1985, who did Thomson remove to claim his 200th and last Test wicket?

20. Which state side did Thomson captain late in his career?

SAMSON'S STATS 2

1. What's the record for the most consecutive ducks in Test cricket?

2. Who holds the record for the most hundreds in consecutive innings with five?

3. What is the most runs scored in a single over in Test cricket?

4. Which batsman holds the record for the most runs in a calendar year, scoring 1788 in 2006?

5. Which Englishman scored the second fastest double century in Test history in 2016?

6. Who holds the record for the highest score on debut with 287 for England v Australia in 1903?

7. Who holds the record for the highest score in a Test by a wicketkeeper with 232 not out v India in 2000?

8. Who holds the record for the highest score by a nightwatchman?

9. Who holds England's record for the highest score by a nightwatchman?

10. Which player holds the record for the most Test runs without scoring a hundred?

11. Who holds the record for having batted most innings (78) before registering a Test-match duck?

12. Which Indian wicketkeeper holds the record for most stumpings in a match (six)?

13. How many players have taken ten wickets and scored a century in the same match?

14. Muttiah Muralitharan holds the record for having taken the most Test wickets on a single ground with 166 wickets at which venue?

15. Whose 7-43 are the best figures for an Englishman on debut?

16. Which English bowler holds the record for being the fastest bowler to take 100 wickets in Tests (16)?

17. Which bowler holds the record for most lbw dismissals in his career (156)?

18. Herbert Ironmonger is the oldest player to take ten wickets in a match, achieving the feat against South Africa in Melbourne in 1932. How old was he?

19. Which Australian bowler took five wickets in six consecutive Test innings in 1888?

20. What record does Aussie left armer Ernie Toshack hold for his 5-2 v India in 1947?

ASHES 2000s

1. What was the result of the 2001 Ashes?

2. Which England pair added 103 for the last wicket in the first Test at Edgbaston?

3. Whose first Ashes century took the game away from England in that match?

4. Which batsman made his debut for England in that Test?

5. Which Australian opener was surprisingly dropped for the last Test of the series?

6. Who was England's player of the series, thanks mainly to a match-winning 173 not out at Headingley in the fourth Test?

7. Who was the stand-in Australian skipper whose declaration gave England the chance to win?

8. Which England seamer made his debut for England in the final Test at the Oval where he allegedly said in response to a slur on his ability from Mark Waugh: 'At least I'm the best player in my family'?

9. Who was Australia's leading wicket taker in that series?

10. Which England batsman retired after the final Test?

11. True or false. Nasser Hussain chose to bat first in the first Ashes Test at Brisbane in 2002–3?

12. Which English seamer injured his knee diving in the outfield on the first day of that match?

13. What were England dismissed for in the final innings of that Test to complete a 384-run defeat?

14. Which England batsman scored 177 in the second Test at Adelaide, his first Ashes century?

15. Name the England batsman who made his debut in that Test, scoring one in each innings.

16. Which England bowler was stretched off after being hit by a ball by Brett Lee in the third Test at Perth?

17. Which Yorkshire seamer was called up for that match to cover for injuries but ended up getting injured himself?

18. Which Queensland batsman made his Test debut for Australia in the fourth Test?

19. Whose 7-94 helped claim a consolation victory in the last Test at Sydney?

20. Which England spinner did Steve Waugh hit for four off the last ball of the day to complete an emotional hometown hundred in Sydney?

ASHES 2005

1. Which Australian fast bowler predicted his side would win the series 5–0?

2. Which England batsman was replaced by Kevin Pietersen for the first Test at Lord's?

3. How many wickets fell on the first day of the first Test at Lord's?

4. Australia won the first Test thanks to Glenn McGrath's bowling but also 91 from which player in his first Ashes Test in the second innings?

5. Which England bowler removed Ponting, Clarke and Warne in Australia's first innings at Edgbaston?

6. Who came in as nightwatchman at the end of the second day for England after Warne had dismissed Strauss with a wickedly spinning delivery?

7. Who gloved behind to give England victory?

8. What was the margin of England's victory?

9.   What feat did Shane Warne achieve in England's first innings at Old Trafford?

10.   Which Australian batsman made a substitute appearance and made two excellent catches to get rid of Pietersen in the first innings and Vaughan in the second?

11.   Off which other player did Geraint Jones acrobatically catch Warne in Australia's second innings?

12.   How many deliveries did McGrath and Lee survive to secure a dramatic draw for Australia?

13.   With whom did Flintoff enjoy a partnership of 177 in England's first innings at Trent Bridge?

14.   Which Australian seamer made his Test debut in this match?

15.   Name the sub fielder who ran out Ricky Ponting in Australia's second innings.

16.   Who hit the winning runs for England?

17.   Who came in to replace Simon Jones for England in the last Test at the Oval?

18.   Which Australian scored a century in Australia's first innings?

19. What was Kevin Pietersen's decisive second innings score which secured England a series-winning draw?

20. Who was the first player to win the Compton–Miller Medal, inaugurated for this series, as man of the series?

TMS GREATS –
RICHARD HADLEE

1. In which New Zealand city was Hadlee born in 1951?

2. What is Hadlee's nickname?

3. For which New Zealand side did Hadlee make his debut in the 1971–2 season?

4. He made his Test-match debut against which side in 1973?

5. What did his first ball in first-class cricket and his first ball in Test cricket have in common?

6. How many wickets did Hadlee take against India in 1976, cementing his place in the side after an uneven start?

7. In 1978 Hadlee's 6-26 helped New Zealand to a historic first win over which side?

8. In 1979–80 Hadlee scored a maiden Test century and 11 wickets in another Test match as New Zealand beat which nation 1–0?

9. How many wickets did Hadlee take in his nation's first win on English soil in 1983?

10. In which year did Hadlee first represent Nottinghamshire?

11. In 1984 Hadlee completed which rare feat for his county?

12. In 1987 he recorded his highest first-class score of 210 against which county?

13. How many times did Notts win the County Championship with Hadlee in their side?

14. Who was Hadlee's captain in both those title-winning seasons?

15. Hadlee excelled with the bat in the 1987 NatWest final, scoring 70 to help Notts beat which side by three wickets?

16. Against which side did Hadlee take 9-52, his best Test figures, in 1985?

17. On 12 November 1988 Hadlee took his 374th Test wicket against India to become the highest wicket taker in Test history. Who did he overtake?

18. At which New Zealand ground did Hadlee claim his 400th Test victim, Sanjay Manjrekar of India, in 1990?

19. Who did Hadlee dismiss for a duck to claim his last Test wicket against England in 1990?

20. In 2002, *Wisden* placed Hadlee in which position among the greatest fast bowlers of all time?
    a) 1st
    b) 2nd
    c) 5th

AGGERS' SEAMERS AND SWINGERS 2

1. Which Surrey and England quick bowler took a hat-trick against the West Indies in 1957?

2. Which county did Ken Higgs play for?

3. Against which nation did John Snow record his best Test figures of 7-40?

4. Michael Holding played for which county between 1983 and 1989?

5. On which bowler did England's Andy Caddick model his action?

6. Against which team did Jimmy Anderson take his 400th Test wicket in 2015?

7. How many Test wickets did Curtly Ambrose take in his career?
   a) 395
   b) 405
   c) 415

8. Who did Darren Gough make his Test debut against?

9. Which county did Neil Foster play for?

10. Which Lancashire seamer, who has taken almost 1,000 first-class wickets, was injured four overs into his one and only international appearance in 2006?

11. Which left-arm seamer won his only cap for England against Pakistan in 1996?

12. Which Aussie seamer who took 94 Test wickets between 2006 and 2009 has the middle name Rupert?

13. Mike Atherton was involved in a famous on-pitch duel against which fast bowler at Trent Bridge in 1998?

14. About which West Indies quick in 1986 did Graham Gooch say it was the only time he had feared for his life on the pitch?

15. Which England swing bowler took a hat-trick in only his third Test for England in 1995?

16. Which Glamorgan player took 2218 wickets, the most of any first-class cricketer to never play a Test?

17. Which batsman did Glenn McGrath dismiss 19 times in his Test career?

18. Name England's bowling coach (as of spring 2016).

19. Which successful Pakistani bowler is said to have 'invented' reverse swing?

20. Which successful English seam bowler wrote a book about the life of a county pro in 1988 called *Eight Days a Week*?

ASHES 2006–7

1. Australia claimed this series 5–0. The first time that had happened since which series?

2. In whose hands at second slip did Steve Harmison's first ball of the first Test at Brisbane end up?

3. Which Australian seamer took six wickets in the match and 4-62 to help claim victory for Australia?

4. Which England batsman was playing in his first Ashes Test?

5. Who scored a double hundred in England's first innings total of 551-6 in the second Test at Adelaide?

6. Who dropped Ricky Ponting early in his inning before he went on to make 142?

7. What was England's overnight score at the end of the fourth day?

8. What were England eventually bowled out for, thanks to Shane Warne's 4-49?

9.   Who scored 61 not out as Australia cruised to a surprising victory by six wickets?

10. Which English spinner came into the side and took 5-92 in the third Test at Perth?

11. How many balls did it take Adam Gilchrist to score a century in Australia's second innings, the fastest in Ashes history and then the second fastest Test hundred of all time?

12. Which England player bagged a pair, his last innings in Test cricket?

13. Which Australian batsman announced his shock retirement after the third Test?

14. The replacement for the player above scored 156 in Australia's one and only innings of the fourth Test at Melbourne, his maiden Test century. Who was he?

15. What landmark did Shane Warne achieve in the fourth Test at Melbourne?

16. Which two players announced they were retiring at the end of the fifth and final Test match at Sydney?

17. Which England player scored 89 in England's first innings, his highest score of the series?

18. Who was McGrath's last Test wicket?

19. Which batsman was given a guard of honour in his last Test innings as Australia cruised to victory once more?

20. With 576 runs, which Australian was named player of the series?

WOMEN'S CRICKET

1. Which English woman holds the record for most runs in a Test career with 1935?

2. Which English woman holds the record for most wickets with 77?

3. Which Australian keeper holds the record for most career dismissals by a wicketkeeper?

4. When was the first women's Test match held?

5. Who played in it?

6. Which English batter scored the first century in women's Test cricket in 1935?

7. Name England women's first Test captain.

8. Which woman scored 179 in 1976 for England against the Australians at the Oval?

9. Which Pakistani batter holds the current record for highest score in a Test-match innings of 242?

10. Who holds the record for England's top score of 189 against New Zealand in February 1935?

11. In a long successful career, what did Charlotte Edwards avoid in 43 Test innings?

12. Which Indian spinner holds the record for the best single innings analysis in Tests of 8-53 against England in 1995?

13. Which Australian player, given the tag the 'Female Bradman', has the lowest career bowling average of any woman to have played Test cricket?

14. Which Australian bowler took the first hat-trick in a woman's Test in 1957?

15. Lindsay Reeler and Denise Annetts share the highest Test partnership in women's cricket history of 309 in 1987 for which side?

16. Which nation registered the lowest total in women's Test cricket history when they were dismissed for 35 in 1957–8?

17. Which New Zealander became the first woman to play 100 ODIs in 1999?

18. Which English woman holds the record for the most number of hundreds in ODIs with nine?

19. In what year were the first ten women admitted into the MCC as members?

20. What new domestic competition for women's cricket was unveiled in February 2016?

ASHES 2009

1. Where was the first Test of the series held?

2. Which batsman joined Sachin Tendulkar, Brian Lara and Allan Border on 11,000 Test runs on his way to 150?

3. Which Australian scored his maiden Test hundred in his side's first innings?

4. How many balls did tenth-wicket pair Jimmy Anderson and Mony Panesar see off to deny Australia victory?

5. Which England announced his decision to retire at the end of the series before the second Test at Lord's?

6. Whose first innings 161 put England in a strong position?

7. Who did Flintoff bowl to win the match and claim his fifth wicket of the innings?

8. This match marked the first time England had won an Ashes Test at Lord's since what year?

9. Which Aussie all rounder was called in to replace Phil Hughes for the third Test?

10. Which Australian batsman scored a third innings ton as the game petered out to a rain-affected draw?

11. England's first innings total at Headingley in the fourth Test was their lowest since 1997 when they were bowled out at Lord's for 77. What was it?

12. Who was their main destroyer with 5-21?

13. Which Aussie scored his second century of the series to put his side in a strong position?

14. Which two players registered the second fastest century partnership in Test history as England fell to a heavy defeat?

15. Name the England batsman who was dropped after four disappointing Tests brought only 105 runs.

16. In the final Test at the Oval whose first innings burst of four wickets for eight runs put England in a healthy position?

17. Who scored a maiden Test century on debut for England in their second innings?

18. Who did Flintoff run out with a direct hit in Australia's second innings?

19. Who caught Hussey at short leg off Graeme Swann to win the Ashes?

20. Who was England's player of the series?

TMS GREATS – MALCOLM MARSHALL

1. On which West Indies island was Marshall born on?

2. What was his nickname?

3. True or false. Marshall was picked to tour India in 1978–9 on the back of two first-class matches.

4. Who was Marshall's first Test wicket?

5. Despite an unsuccessful tour, which English county was willing to sign him for the 1979 season?

6. Which fellow West Indian bowler did he succeed at Hampshire?

7. Against which side did Marshall take 7-24 in 1980?

8. Despite this, and due to the West Indies bowling strength, Marshall was dropped. When was he recalled?

9. Who did Marshall make his highest Test score of 92 against 1984?

10. What was remarkable about Marshall's 7-53 v England at Headingley in 1984?

11. On which English ground did Marshall complete his best Test figures of 7-22 in 1988?

12. Which England batsman did Marshall dismiss 16 times in Tests?

13. Which England batsman said this of Marshall: 'He was one of the major reasons I moved to Hampshire for the last two years of my career: the chance to play with him for once, not against him'?

14. Which county did Marshall claim his best first-class figures of 8-71 against in 1982?

15. True or false. Marshall's bowling average of 20.94 is the best of any bowler who has taken more than 200 Test wickets.

16. In what year did he play his last Test?

17. Who was his final, 376th Test wicket?

18. Marshall scored 29 and took three wickets in the 1992 Benson and Hedges final as Hampshire beat which side?

19. In what year did he become coach of Hampshire and the West Indies?

20. In what year did Marshall sadly die of cancer?

TUFFERS' TWIRLERS 2

1. After Jim Laker, which Indian spinner has the best match figures in Test history (16-136) against West Indies in 1988?

2. Which England slow left armer has the best career strike rate of any spinner in Test history, achieved between 1884 and 1899?

3. How many times did Derek Underwood take 100 wickets in a first-class season?

4. Who took the only other Australian wicket in 'Laker's Match' at Old Trafford in 1956?

5. Which county was Jim Laker born in?

6. Which Indian spinner took more Test wickets (242) than he scored runs (167)?

7. Which England off spinner did Brian Lara hit for four to reach his world record 400 not out in Antigua in 2004?

8. In which country was spinner Peter Such born?

9.   Which English spinner has the third worst career bowling average in Test history (minimum 2000 deliveries) of 76.95?

10.   Which English county did John Mortimore play for?

11.   Which West Indian batsman did Richard Illingworth get out with his first ball in Test cricket in 1991?

12.   Which Australian one-day specialist batsman also took 29 Test wickets bowling left-arm Chinamen?

13.   Which Pakistani slow left armer, who took 171 Test wickets, has the lowest economy rate of any spinner his country has produced?

14.   Which English leg spinner was voted PCA Young Player of the Year in 2007?

15.   What is John Emburey's middle name?

16.   Between 1960 and 1966, which England off spinner took 122 wickets in 39 Tests and was unlucky not to play more?

17.   Which Yorkshire off spinner played in three Tests in Pakistan in 1977–8 after having remodelled his action because it was deemed suspect?

18.   Who holds the world record for the most Test wickets by a left-arm spinner?

19. After Muttiah Muralitharan, who holds the record for the most Test wickets taken by an off spinner?

20. How many wickets did Phil Tufnell take in his debut Test against Australia in Melbourne in 1990?

ASHES 2010–1

1. Which bowler took a hat-trick on the opening day of the 2010–1 series in Brisbane?

2. Who was dismissed for the hat-trick ball?

3. Which pair did Andrew Strauss and Alastair Cook overcome to become England's most successful opening partnership during their first wicket stand of 188?

4. Whose Test record at the Gabba did Cook surpass with his 235 not out?

5. Which Australian batsman was run out without facing a ball on the first morning of the second Test at Adelaide?

6. What record had Alastair Cook broken when he ended day two unbeaten on 136?

7. Which player scored a Test best of 227 as England went on to post 620-5 declared?

8. Which part timer removed Michael Clarke late on the fourth day for 80?

9. Which England bowler achieved his first five-wicket haul against Australia to bowl his side to victory on the fourth day?

10. Which Aussie batsman made his Ashes debut for Australia in the third Test at Perth?

11. Name the England seamer who replaced Stuart Broad and took eight wickets in the match.

12. Whose second innings hundred, the only of the match, turned the match in Australia's favour?

13. Which Aussie took six wickets to reduce England to 123 all out and level the series?

14. What score did England bowl Australia out for on day one of the fourth Test at Melbourne?

15. Which England batsman scored his fifth Test century in England's first innings of 513?

16. True or false. The losses at Adelaide and Melbourne marked the first time Australia had ever lost two Tests in a home series by an innings.

17. Usman Khawaja made his Test debut for Australia in the fifth and final Test at Sydney. Which other Aussie was playing his first Test?

18. Two England players registered their first Ashes hundreds in England's first innings 644. Ian Bell was one. Who was the other?

19. England's 3–1 series victory was their first in Australia since which series?

20. Alastair Cook was player of the series. How many runs did he amass in the series?

TMS GREATS – ALLAN BORDER

1.   In which Australian state was Border born?

2.   When did he make his first-class debut?

3.   In 1977 Border played one first-class match for which English county?

4.   Who did he make his Test debut against in 1978?

5.   Who was Border's first Test wicket?

6.   Against which side did he notch the first of 27 Test centuries in March 1979?

7.   For his stout resistance during the 1982 Ashes, Border was given which coveted accolade?

8.   Who did he succeed as Australian skipper in 1984?

9.   Which state side did Border play for from 1980?

10. Where did Border score an unbeaten 146 to prevent Australia sliding to defeat in the 1985 Ashes?

11. The appointment of which coach helped Border reverse Australian's miserable run of Test form in the 1980s?

12. Winning what trophy in 1987 heralded the start of a victorious era for Australia?

13. Who did Border's highest Test score of 205 in 1987–8 come against?

14. Which team did Border achieve his best Test figures of 7-46 against in 1989?

15. What order did Border give his team ahead of the 1989 Ashes?

16. In which country did Border record his only Test series victory on the subcontinent in 1992?

17. Which West Indies bowler dashed Border's hope of winning a series against the West Indies when he removed Craig McDermott within two runs of victory?

18. Whose record for most Test runs did Border pass in 1993?

19. Against which side did Border play his last Test in 1994?

20. How many Test matches did Border play?
    a) 146
    b) 156
    c) 166

ASHES 2013

1. By what score did England win the series?

2. Which Aussie spinner made his debut in the first Test at Trent Bridge but made a greater mark with the bat?

3. Which England player refused to walk after nicking to slip in England's second innings and wasn't given out, and Australia had used up all their reviews?

4. Who did Jimmy Anderson remove to win the game for England with Australia 14 runs short?

5. Two Yorkshire batsmen were playing in their first Ashes Test. One was Joe Root. Who was the other?

6. Whose 180 in the second Test at Lord's was his maiden Ashes hundred?

7. Australia's first innings 128 was their lowest total at Lord's since what year?

8. How many wickets did Graeme Swann take in England's 347-run win at Lord's?

9. Which Australian batsman made his first Ashes appearance in the third Test at Old Trafford?

10. Whose 113 in England's first innings marked his last Ashes hundred?

11. Where was the fourth Test of the series played?

12. Which Aussie bowler made his Ashes debut in that match?

13. Who scored their maiden Test century in that match at the age of 35?

14. Which England batsman scored his third century of the series, which would see him being named England's player of the series?

15. How many runs were Australia chasing for victory in the fourth innings?

16. Who took 6-20 in 45 balls to win the match for England on the fourth day?

17. England named two debutants for the fifth and final Test at the Oval. Simon Kerrigan was one. Who was the other?

18. Which player was making his Australian Test debut?

19. Why did England's run chase end with them 21 runs short of victory, with four overs remaining?

20. Who was named Australia's player of the series?

ASHES 2013–4

1. Australia won this series to make it how many clean sweeps in Ashes history?

2. Why was this series only held three months after the end of the previous series in England?

3. Mitchell Johnson destroyed England with 37 wickets in this series. How many did he claim in the first Test?

4. Who made his Ashes debut as opener for England in the first Test at Brisbane?

5. Which batsman recorded his maiden Ashes ton in Australia's second innings?

6. Who made his Test debut for England in the second Test at Adelaide?

7. Who top scored for England in their second innings with 87 as they slid to a second heavy defeat?

8. Who was named man of the match for Australia?

9. Where was the third Test of the series played?

10. That Test marked Michael Clarke's 100th Test. Which other player reached the same landmark in that Test?

11. Whose first innings 111 set Australia up for a score of 385?

12. Ben Stokes recorded his maiden Test hundred in England's second innings. Who did he pull for four to reach his century?

13. Which player retired before the fourth Test at Melbourne?

14. England were in a powerful position after the first innings, but whose 5-50 dragged Australia back into it?

15. Which spinner was making his 50th Test appearance for England?

16. Mitchell Johnson was named man of the match. How many times did he win the award in that series?

17. Three players made their Test debut for England in the last Test in Sydney? Gary Ballance, Scott Borthwick and which other player?

18. Which England player recorded his first five-wicket haul in Australia's first innings?

19. True or false. Australia named the same team in every Test.

20. Who was England's highest scorer in the series with 294 runs?

ASHES 2015

1. Which Australian retired before the start of the series with a knee injury?

2. Who was called in to replace him?

3. Who dropped Joe Root in England's first innings in the first Test at Cardiff, before he went on to score 134?

4. Which Australian batsman started that Test ranked as the best in the world?

5. Who became the first batsman to record seven consecutive Test half-centuries without converting one to a hundred?

6. Who opened the batting with Alastair Cook in this Test and for the rest of the series?

7. Who replaced Brad Haddin as keeper for the second Test at Lord's?

8. For what score did England capitulate in their second innings to allow Australia to draw level in the series?

9. Which player became the second after Shane Warne to reach 300 wickets and 2000 Test runs in the third Test at Edgbaston?

10. Who was instrumental in bowling Australia out for 136 on the first day of that match with 6-47?

11. Whose late order 59 gave England a crucial first innings cushion?

12. Whose six wickets in Australia's second innings put England on the verge of victory, earning him the man of the match award ?

13. What were Australia bowled out for in the first innings at Trent Bridge?

14. How many overs did their innings last, the least ever in the first innings of a Test match?

15. What were Stuart Broad's remarkable figures, the best ever by a fast bowler in an Ashes Test?

16. What was the highest score in Australia's innings?

17. Which England player became the second after Ian Botham to have played in five Ashes-winning sides?

18. Two Australian players announced their retirement after this match. Chris Rogers and who else?

19. Who won the Compton–Miller Medal for player of the series?

20. As things stand, who was won more Test matches in Ashes history, England or Australia?

BLOWER'S KEEPERS

1. Which English keeper was the first to reach 200 Test dismissals?

2. Which England keeper was the first to record 2000 runs and 100 Test dismissals?

3. Which South African keeper holds the record for the highest score (182) and the most dismissals in an innings (6) in the same match?

4. What is the highest number of stumpings a keeper has ever taken in a Test series?
   a) 8
   b) 9
   c) 10

5. Which England keeper became the first to take 11 catches in a match against South Africa in Johannesburg in 1995?

6. Four keepers have taken seven dismissals in a Test-match innings. Which Pakistani keeper was the first in 1979?

7. Which West Indian keeper became the latest in 2000?

8. Who is the only England wicketkeeper to take seven dismissals, against India in 1980?

9. Which English keeper holds the record for taking the most stumpings in a first-class career with 418?

10. Who holds the record for taking the most catches with 1473?

11. What is the world record for the number of dismissals in an innings in first-class cricket?
    a) 8
    b) 9
    c) 10

12. Three English keepers have taken eight dismissals in an innings in first-class cricket. Which Essex keeper was the first in 1985 against Somerset?

13. Which Surrey keeper was the third and latest to do it in 2004 at the Oval against Kent?

14. Who holds the record for most dismissals in an ODI career?

15. Who holds the record for most catches in an ODI career?

16. Which Australian wicketkeeper refused to run out Fred Titmus after he collided with Neil Hawke and was stranded out of his ground in 1964?

17.   Which English keeper had a run in the Test side which involved him playing in 89 out of a possible 93 Tests?

18.   Which Australian keeper broke Rod Marsh's world record of 355 Test dismissals in 1998?

19.   In 1981 John Arlott selected which Somerset wicketkeeper as the finest never to play for England?

20.   True or false. West Indies wicketkeeper David Murray was the brother of Deryck Murray.

TMS GREATS – WASIM AND WAQAR

1. Where was Wasim born in 1966?

2. In what year did Wasim make his first-class debut?

3. Against which team did he make his Test debut in that same year?

4. How many wickets did he take in his second Test to win man of the match?
   a) 8
   b) 10
   c) 12

5. Against which team did Wasim take his Test best of 7-119 in 1994?

6. Who did he score his Test best score of 257 not out against in 1996?

7. At which World Cup final did Wasim win man of the match?

8. When was he made Pakistan captain?

9.   Which English county did Wasim join in 1988?

10.   Which Test great, after his retirement in 2012, said along with Curtly Ambrose Wasim was the toughest bowler he'd faced?

11.   What year was Waqar Younis born?

12.   What year did he make his Test debut against India?

13.   Which player was also making his debut for India?

14.   Against which side did Waqar take his best Test figures of 7-76 in Faisalabad in 1990?

15.   For what reason was Waqar removed from the attack in the World Cup match against Australia in 2003?

16.   True or false. Waqar was captain at the time.

17.   Who did he play his last Test against in January 2003?

18.   Against which side did Waqar complete a hat-trick in an ODI in 1994?

19.   Which English county did Waqar play for between 1990 and 1993?

20.   What position in the Pakistani cricket team was Waqar appointed to in 2007?

TEA

VIEW FROM
THE BOUNDARY

1. Which English female pop star did Aggers entertain in the box in 2009?

2. When did Prime Minister David Cameron drop into the *TMS* box?

3. Which politician admitted to having been in the crowd when Geoff Boycott scored his 100th hundred at Headingley in 1977?

4. The film-star cousin of a pair of New Zealand cricketing brothers visited the box in July 2009. Name him.

5. Which child film star and cricket fan was referred to by a vexed Boycott as 'that bloody little wizard'?

6. Which cricket-loving, piano-playing singer-songwriter confessed he was too nervous to watch the end of the second Test of the 2005 Ashes at Edgbaston?

7. Which member of the Stranglers played 'Golden Brown' in the *TMS* box, prompting Aggers to tell Mike Selvey that was what a real guitar sounded like?

8. Which comedian and actor described cricket as a 'hard, sharp, fast game' during his 'View from the Boundary' (VFTB) interview in 2002?

9. Which unlikely political guest did Henry Blofeld interview in 2000?

10. Which South African cleric and peace activist visited the box and did a spot of commentary in 1994?

11. What year was Brian Johnston's last VFTB?

12. In his last interview, with comedian Roy Hudd, what favourite song of Brian Johnston's did the pair duet on?

13. In 1991, which player in his last Test did actor Peter O'Toole describe as 'The Great King'?

14. Which Monty Python star told Jonners in 1990 that he often saw him in his local off-licence?

15. Which cricket-loving prime minister gave an interview in which he admitted that, as a minister, he was often passed cricket scores during boring meetings?

16. Rory Bremner was surprised in 1985 when which commentator, a subject of his impersonation, burst in and demanded 'where are the royalties?'

17. Which novelist, playwright and screenwriter guest in 1980 said that he seen W.G. Grace play and saw Bradman make his Test debut?

18. Which living member of the royal family has appeared on VFTB?

19. Which Yorkshire-born chat-show host and journalist appeared on VFTB in 1987?

20. Which *TMS* commentator took over the regular slot of interviewing guests after Johnners's death?

MIDDLE NAMES

Name the cricketer from his middle name:

1. Sewards.

2. Terence.

3. Ramesh.

4. Barrie.

5. Nathan.

6. Willem.

7. Verity.

8. Devereux.

9. Sharad.

10. Ivon.

11. Henri.

12. Bale.

13. Clarence.

14. Verdon.

15. Maclean.

16. Chokshanada.

17. Luca.

18. Leslie.

19. St Aubrun.

20. Ravin.

CRICKET TERMS 2

Give the terms for the following:

1. To be palpably lbw.

2. A ball that doesn't spin.

3. A ball that is caught but has gone straight into the ground after being hit.

4. Where a batsman fails to ground his bat in the popping crease while running.

5. A catching position halfway or so to the third-man boundary.

6. When a batsman is out he is said to be 'Back in the...?'

7. An exceptionally good ball.

8. The place where a batsman always looks good.

9. Another term for an edge.

10. A ball that doesn't bounce as high as the batsman expected.

11.   To insult or 'mentally disintegrate' the opposition.

12.   Another term for googly: the ball that goes the other way.

13.   Comes after nine, ten…?

14.   A period of bowling.

15.   A ball hit very high for a catch.

16.   The weakest part of the batting order.

17.   Given out by an over-eager umpire.

18.   An over in which no runs are scored.

19.   A placid batting pitch offering no help to any bowler.

20.   A shot that invariably ends up in 'cow corner' if a batsman connects.

LOOK IN THE BOOK 2

Who wrote the following autobiographies?

1.   *Playing with Fire.*

2.   *What Now?*

3.   *Anything But an Autobiography.*

4.   *You Guys Are History!*

5.   *Dazzler.*

6.   *Opening Up.*

7.   *Behind the Shades.*

8.   *Line and Strength.*

9.   *No Holding Back.*

10.   *The Breaks Are Off.*

11.   *Playing it My Way.*

12. *Sunny Days.*

13. *White Lightning.*

14. *Anything But Murder.*

15. *Menace.*

16. *Third Man to Fatty's Leg.*

17. *Playing for Keeps.*

18. *Coming Back to Me.*

19. *True Colours.*

20. *Strictly Me – My Life Under the Spotlight.*

NAME THE PLAYER 3

Name the player from their nickname:

1. Picca.

2. Ramps.

3. All Hands.

4. Barnacle.

5. Rowdy.

6. The Postman.

7. Dickie.

8. Zulu.

9. The Gnome.

10. Butch.

11. Pistol.

12. Kipper.

13. Viru.

14. Spiro.

15. Boof.

16. Skid.

17. Swampy.

18. Daffy.

19. Colonel.

20. Mr Cricket.

FOOTBALL
AND CRICKET

1. Which 1966 World Cup hero played one first-class match for Essex in 1962?

2. Which England, Leicestershire and Yorkshire player played for Carlisle United, Doncaster Rovers and Huddersfield Town?

3. Name the last double international to represent his country at football and cricket.

4. Which colourful cricketer played one match for England at full back in 1901 and 26 Test matches as well as having a successful athletics and rugby union career?

5. Who did Les Ames play five games for in the 1931 season?

6. Three men have represented Yorkshire and England at cricket and also played for Bradford City. Brian Close and Ken Taylor are two. Name the other.

7. England player and later coach Micky Stewart played for which London side?

8. Which Yorkshire and England bowler also played for Manchester United?

9. Middlesex and England great Patsy Hendren played for four different football sides. Name one.

10. Which Worcestershire captain was witness to the tragic fire at Bradford City in 1985 which claimed the lives of 56 fans because he was playing for their opponents Lincoln City?

11. Which cricketer's last game of football was the 1950 FA Cup final?

12. Which fast bowler combined appearances for Middlesbrough and Yorkshire CC between 1975 and 1980?

13. Which striker played for the MCC against Germany at Lord's, was out for a single but quipped: 'I always score against the Germans'?

14. Which footballing brothers played together for Lancashire's under 14s team?

15. Which successful county batsman turned to professional cricket with Glamorgan and then Sussex after being released by Swansea after three professional appearances?

16. Who is the only man to have captained England at both cricket and football?

17. Which West Indian great is reported to have played a World Cup qualifier for Antigua in 1974?

18. Name Denis Compton's brother who played for Arsenal and Middlesex.

19. The nephew of which former England captain played 44 times for Brighton and Hove Albion before signing for Sussex?

20. Which former England fast bowler became manager of Ashington in 2014?

NAME THE GROUND 2

Name the grounds which have (or had) the following stands, ends or landmarks:

1.   Mound Stand.

2.   Western Terrace.

3.   Chappell Stands (demolished).

4.   Eric Hollies Stand.

5.   Three Ws Stand.

6.   Sir Ian Botham Stand.

7.   Diglis End.

8.   Brian Statham End.

9.   Ponsford Stand.

10.   Les Ames Stand.

11. Bill O'Reilly Stand.

12. Grace Gates.

13. Hobbs Gate.

14. Vijay Merchant Stand.

15. Lumley End.

16. River Taff End.

17. Wantage Road End.

18. Inverarity Stand.

19. Sea End.

20. Bennett End.

GUESS THE COACH

1. Who was the first man to be appointed England cricket coach in 1986?

2. Who is the only man to have held the England coach's position twice?

3. Which former Yorkshire captain served as coach and 'supremo' between 1995 and 1996?

4. Which former player was an umpire, then a commentator, before going into coaching and held the England job between 1996 and 1999?

5. Who is the longest serving England coach?

6. Who was appointed to the role in 2015?

7. Which former Aussie spinner was credited with developing Shane Warne's talent?

8. Which Australian Test player has led Yorkshire to two consecutive County Championship wins?

9. Which coach is widely recognized as having transformed a failing Australian side when he took charge in 1986?

10. Which Test player did John Buchanan replace as Australian coach in 1999?

11. Which Australian was the West Indies fitness coach during their 1980s heyday?

12. Who is the current coach of the West Indies?

13. Which former Australian opener coached Sri Lanka between 2003 and 2005 and then the West Indies between 2007 and 2009?

14. Which South African was coach of the Indian side in their successful 2011 World Cup campaign?

15. Which Aussie great enjoyed a turbulent two-year spell as coach of the Indian cricket team between 2005 and 2007?

16. Name the Australian who coached Sri Lanka to the final of the 2007 World Cup.

17. Dav Whatmore has coached Sri Lanka, Bangladesh and Pakistan. Who does he currently coach?

18. Which English coach of Pakistan died during the 2007 World Cup?

19. Which county side does Ashley Giles currently coach?

20. Which former South African, Kent and Surrey coach is in his second stint as head coach of the Sri Lankan team?

BEST OF BEARDERS 3

1. The highest team score in first-class cricket, achieved by Victoria v New South Wales in 1926, is?
   a) 1059
   b) 1107
   c) 1197

2. Which West Indian fast bowler sent down 15 balls in an over against Australia in Perth in 1996–7, widely believed to be the longest ever?

3. The record for the most consecutive maidens bowled was achieved by R.G. Nadkarni for India against England at Madras in 1964. How many did he bowl?
   a) 21
   b) 23
   c) 25

4. Which England bowler was the last Test cricketer to take four wickets in an over, against the West Indies in 2000?

5.   How many instances have there been of all 11 players on the field bowling in a Test match?
     a) 4
     b) 5
     c) 6

6.   True or false. Batsmen have to inform the umpire if they are changing their bowling style (e.g. from medium pace to spin)?

7.   Which Indian bowler, with 27, has the most number of caught and bowleds in Test cricket?

8.   True or false. Bradman only averaged 27 at Old Trafford.

9.   What is the cheapest ten-wicket haul in first-class cricket history?

10. Who is the only Test batsman to have twice scored a hundred runs before lunch?

11. Who is the youngest man to have scored a century for England?

12. Who is the old man to have scored a hundred in Test match cricket?

13. Which Kent batsman and later an umpire became the only man in first-class cricket history to score a double century in each innings of a match in 1938 v Essex?

14. Name the only Welshman to captain England at cricket.

15. Which Lancashire skipper was given the man of the match award purely for his captaincy in a Benson and Hedges Cup final?

16. Which Warwickshire spinner once took all ten wickets without the aid of any fielder: seven bowled, three lbw?

17. What is the record for the most wickets to have fallen in a day of first-class cricket?
     a) 38
     b) 39
     c) 40

18. Which English county holds the record for having the most players in an England team at one time with six?

19. Which Yorkshireman with 146 holds the record for the highest score in a domestic one-day final?

20. True or false. When England played Australia in 1979, Lillee was caught Willey bowled Dilley in the gully.

TROUBLE AND STRIFE

1. Which former England captain landed himself in trouble on tour in Australia by buzzing the ground in a Tiger Moth plane in 1991?

2. Who was the other player in the plane?

3. Which two Australian players betted their team would lose in Headingley in 1981 at odds of 500–1?

4. Which South African captain was banned for life for his role in match-fixing and later died in a plane crash?

5. Which Australian spinner was banned for a year in 2003 after testing positive for a banned substance, which he said was a diet pill given to him by his mother?

6. Which England all rounder was banned after he admitted to smoking cannabis in 1986?

7. Which Pakistani captain was jailed for 30 months and banned for 10 years for his role in a spot-fixing scandal in England in 2010?

8. Which former Indian captain was banned for life for his role in a match-fixing scandal?

9. Which Australian cricketer was sent home from the World Twenty20 Cup in 2012 for an 'alcohol-related incident'?

10. Which England cricketer was reported to be seen riding a pedalo in the wee small hours of the morning under the influence of alcohol at the 2007 World Cup?

11. Which former England captain skippered a highly controversial rebel tour to South Africa in 1989–90?

12. What is it alleged that England players threw on the pitch during the 2007 Oval Test against India?

13. Which West Indies fast-bowling great kicked over the stumps in frustration at umpiring decisions during his side's 1979–80 tour of New Zealand?

14. Name the England opener, now a match referee, who demolished his stumps with his bat after being dismissed against Australia in 1988.

15. With which former Australian captain is Ian Botham said to have enjoyed a feud lasting 38 years?

16. Which Pakistani cricketer was banned for a Test match and two ODIs after apparently trying to rough up the pitch against England in 2006?

17. Which England captain was fined heavily for the 'Dirt in the Pocket Affair' in 1994?

18. Which Zimbabwe batsman was banned from the game for a year for allegedly throwing a ball at a spectator who heckled him in a league game?

19. Which bowler played four Tests for England after returning from an 18-month ban for testing positive for cocaine in 1996?

20. Which Yorkshire captain was banned from lifting his side's trophy after they won the County Championship in 2014 for comments he'd made to Ashwell Prince in a previous match?

CRICKET FIRSTS

Name the player:

1. First player to score 10,000 runs in Tests.

2. First bowler to take 100 Test wickets.

3. First batsman to score a Test-match century.

4. First all rounder to take 100 wickets and score a 1000 runs.

5. First triple century in Tests.

6. First quadruple century in first-class cricket.

7. First hat-trick in Tests.

8. First duck in Test history.

9. First ten wickets in an innings in Test cricket.

10. First batsman to hit the first ball of a Test for six.

11. First batsman to score a century Test debut.

12.   First batsman to score a 100 first-class centuries.

13.   First man to play in 100 Tests

14.   First wicketkeeper to take 300 dismissals.

15.   First bowler to take 400 wickets

16.   First bowler to take 500 wickets.

17.   First player to take 100 catches in tests.

18.   First batsman to score 500 in an innings in first-class cricket.

19.   First batsman to score a double century in an ODI.

20.   First bowler to take a wicket with their first ball in Test cricket.

EVENING SESSION

TMS GREATS – SHANE WARNE

1. In which state of Australia was Warne born in 1969?

2. What other sport did the young Warne play to a high level?

3. Which Lancashire League team did Warne play for in 1991, though they decided not to re-engage him for the following season because he wasn't deemed good enough?

4. Which coach and former Australian player is credited with transforming and mentoring Warne as a leg-spin bowler?

5. How many wickets did Warne take on debut for Victoria in 1991?

6. How many Sheffield Shield matches had Warne played for Victoria before he was selected to play for Australia in the third Test against India in January 1992?

7. On an otherwise fruitless debut, who was Warne's first Test wicket?

8. Where did Warne kickstart his Test career by taking 7-52 against the West Indies, and so win man of the match?

9. How many wickets did Warne take in the six-Test Ashes series in England in 1993?

10. Who was at the non-striker's end as Warne fizzed his first ball in Ashes cricket past Mike Gatting's defence?

11. What Test record did Warne break in 1993?

12. Against which team did Warne achieve his best Test figures of 8-71 at Brisbane?

13. Which South African batsman became known as Warne's 'bunny', having been dismissed by him 12 times, including Tests and ODIs?

14. Which batsman did he dismiss most in Test-match cricket?

15. Who did Warne dismiss to complete a hat-trick against England at the MCG in 1994?

16. What was Warne's highest score with the bat in Test cricket?

17. Which English county did Warne join in 2000?

18. Name the Indian Premier League team Warne played for between 2011 and 2013.

19. When did Warne play his last Test?

20. True or false. Warne was a captain on BBC's *Question of Sport* in 2007.

SAMSON'S STATS 3

1. Who currently holds the record for the most ODI runs in a career with 18,426?

2. Who holds the current record of highest score in an ODI innings with 264?

3. What's the highest innings total in an ODI, scored by Sri Lanka in 2006 v Netherlands?

4. What's the lowest total, achieved by Zimbabwe against Sri Lanka in 2004?

5. Which Pakistani holds the record for hitting most sixes in an ODI career?

6. Who holds the record for hitting most sixes in a single innings with 16?

7. Which Pakistani batsman has scored 5122 ODI runs but never scored a hundred?

8. Who scored the fastest hundred in ODI history off 31 balls v the West Indies in Johannesburg in 2015?

9. Which West Indies player currently has the highest strike rate of any player in ODI history of 130.81?

10. Who is currently England's highest run scorer in ODIs with 5416?

11. Who with 269 has taken most wickets?

12. Which team scored 438 in 49.5 overs to beat Australia in 2006, the highest run chase in ODI history?

13. Who did England score 408-9 against at Edgbaston to record their highest ever ODI score?

14. Who holds the record for the most wickets in an ODI career with 534?

15. Which Sri Lanka bowler has the best ODI figures, 8-19 against Zimbabwe in 2001?

16. Which Pakistani bowler has conceded the most runs in an ODI career?

17. Which West Indies bowler has the best career economy rate in ODIs with 3.09?

18. Which Irishman has the worst economy rate in a single innings when he carted for 95 off seven overs against South Africa in 2015?

19.   Which Pakistani bowler took the first ODI hat-trick in 1982 against Australia?

20.   Who scored the first ever ODI hundred, for England v Australia in 1973?

296

WORLD CUP 1975

1. Where was the 1975 World Cup held?

2. Who was its sponsor?

3. How many teams took part?

4. Beyond the six then Test teams, who were the other two sides?

5. England won their opening match, beating India by 202 runs thanks to a century by which batsman?

6. Which Indian batsman batted through his side's innings and finished on 36 not out?

7. New Zealand qualified with England from Group A. Who was their captain?

8. Which Essex batsman's ton helped England beat New Zealand and top their group?

9. Who took 4-20 for the West Indies in their opening match as they skittled Sri Lanka for 86?

10. The West Indies won their second match in thrilling fashion when they were 203-9 chasing Pakistan's 266, but won with two balls to spare. Which two players pulled off that incredible victory?

11. Australia qualified with them from Group B. Who scored a century for them to beat Sri Lanka in their second match?

12. Which team topped Group B: West Indies or Australia?

13. Where did the semi-final between England and Australia take place?

14. Which Australian bowler took 6-14 as England were bundled out for 93?

15. Who scored 72 for the West Indies as they cruised to a five-wicket win against New Zealand at the Oval?

16. Which West Indies batsman hooked Dennis Lillee for six but trod on his stumps in doing so?

17. Who kept centurion Clive Lloyd company in a fourth wicket stand of 149?

18. Which Australian batsman was the third of Viv Richards's three run outs, chancing a run on a misfield when he was on 62?

19. How was Jeff Thomson dismissed to give the West Indies victory by 17 runs?

20. Who was the World Cup's highest run scorer with 333 runs?

WORLD SERIES
CRICKET

1. Who was the media mogul behind World Series Cricket?

2. What was the name of the TV network he owned?

3. What year did the first World Series matches take place?

4. Unable to use the words 'Test match', what did the organizers use instead?

5. Who contested the first match in December 1977?

6. Whose jaw was broken in the Sydney match by an Andy Roberts bouncer?

7. What new piece of protective equipment is believed to have developed as a direct result of that incident?

8. As well as day-night cricket, what other innovation did the World Series introduce?

9. Who won that three-match series 2–1?

10.   Who captained the West Indies side?

11.   Which Australian scored the first century in World Series
      Cricket at Adelaide in the third match of that series?

12.   Which West Indies great followed suit in that match?

13.   Who captained the World XI for the one-day tournament in
      1977 and 1978?

14.   Which West Indies bowler took five wickets in the final of that
      tournament to give them victory?

15.   In 1978–9, Australia and the West Indies took on a World
      XI in a tripartite Test-match tournament. Who captained the
      World XI?

16.   Which England keeper kept wicket for the World side?

17.   Which fearsome South African seamer took five wickets as they
      defeated the host nation in Melbourne?

18.   Which South African opener scored an unbeaten hundred as
      the World XI beat Australia by five wickets?

19.   In which country was the 1978 one-day tournament held?

20.   In what year did World Series Cricket end?

TMS GREATS – THE CHAPPELLS

1. Who is older: Greg or Ian?

2. In a suburb of which Australian city were they born and raised?

3. Which other sport did Ian excel at as a boy?

4. Which state did Ian make his debut for in 1962?

5. Who was captain of the New South Wales team which Ian scored his maiden first-class century against?

6. In 1963 Ian played a single first-class match for which county side?

7. True or false. When Ian was selected for the Test team he was considered as an all rounder for his leg spin.

8. Which side did Ian make his maiden Test century against at Melbourne in 1967–8 to save his place in the side?

9. Who did Ian succeed as Australian captain in 1971?

10. At which English ground in the 1972 Ashes did Ian and Greg become the first brothers to score centuries in the same Test innings?

11. Who did Ian score his highest Test score of 196 against in 1972–3?

12. When did Ian play his last Test match?

13. Whose place did Greg take in the South Australia team when he was 18?

14. Which English county did Greg play for in 1968 and 1969?

15. Greg scored a debut century against England at Perth in 1970. With whom did he share a stand of 219?

16. Which esteemed commentator rated Greg's 131 v England in 'Massie's Test' in 1972 'close to the most flawless innings I had seen'?

17. Who did Greg take best Test figures of 5-61 against in 1972–3?

18. Against which side did Greg register his Test best score of 247 not out in 1974?

19. Greg scored the highest individual score in World Series Cricket. Was it?
    a) 246
    b) 256
    c) 266

20. What record did Greg achieve in his final Test in 1984?

WORLD CUP 1979

1.   Where was the World Cup held?

2.   How many overs per side were the matches?

3.   As well as Sri Lanka, who were the other non Test-playing nation to make up the field of eight?

4.   Who won the opening match in Group A between England and Australia?

5.   Who took most wickets for England in that match with two?

6.   In their second match England bowled Canada out for 45. Who did the damage with 4-11 in 10.3 overs?

7.   Who beat Australia in their second match to knock them out of the tournament?

8.   Whose unbeaten hundred saw the West Indies coast to victory over India in their first match in Group B?

9.   Whose unbeaten 84 saw New Zealand cruise to a decisive victory against India in their second match?

10. Where was the first semi-final between England and New Zealand held?

11. Who was the only surviving England player from their semi-final defeat to Australia four years before?

12. Who top scored for England with 71 in their total of 221-8?

13. Who brilliantly ran out John Wright for 69 as England sneaked into the final by nine runs?

14. Which new opening partner helped Greenidge add 132 for the first wicket in the second semi-final between West Indies and Pakistan?

15. Pakistan were well placed at 176-1 before collapsing. Whose 93 put them in that strong position?

16. Who did Randall run out to give England an early scalp in the final?

17. Viv Richards's 138 set the tone. But whose 86 from 77 balls took the game even further away from England?

18. With whom did Geoff Boycott share a century opening partnership that many deemed to be too slow?

19. Who took five wickets to clean up the England innings and give the Windies their second World Cup?

20. Who was the tournament's leading wicket taker with 10?

WORLD CUP 1983

1.   Where was the World Cup held?

2.   Who were the only one of the eight teams not to have Test status?

3.   What format change was made for this tournament?

4.   Who scored a ton for England in their opening match against New Zealand at the Oval?

5.   At which ground hosting its first international match did David Gower score 130 as England racked up 333 against Sri Lanka?

6.   Who finished second behind England to qualify from Group A?

7.   Who captained the Zimbabwe side in their memorable victory over Australia in the nation's first World Cup game, scored 69 not out and took 4-42?

8.   Who scored 89 as India upset the holders West Indies, their first World Cup defeat, in their opening game?

9.   Which Windies bowler took 7-51 as they routed Australia at Leeds?

10. Whose 119 at the Oval gave the West Indies victory over India in their second match and assured them top place in their group?

11. Whose 32-ball 51 saw India to a semi-final victory over the hosts at Old Trafford?

12. Where was the semi-final between Pakistan and the West Indies held?

13. Which batsman was missing for Pakistan with 'flu as they lost their third successive World Cup semi?

14. Which batsman contributed useful overs as the first bowler for the West Indies throughout the tournament, and took 2-49 from 11 overs in the final v India?

15. Who top scored for India in their 183 all out?

16. Name the seamer who bowled Greenidge as he shouldered arms for one.

17. Whose running catch to dismiss Viv Richards for 33 was seen as a turning point in the match?

18. Which part-time seamer took 3-12 off seven overs to win man of the match as the Windies middle order crumbled?

19.   Whose 175 not out against Zimbabwe at Tunbridge Wells was a World Cup record, beating Glenn Turner's 171 v East Africa in 1975?

20.   Who was the World Cup's leading wicket taker?

WORLD CUP 1987

1. In which two countries was the 1987 World Cup held?

2. Who was its sponsor?

3. The length of matches was reduced from 60 to how many overs?

4. Who did hosts India lose to in their opening match, despite only needing 15 from the last four overs?

5. Whose 142 against New Zealand nearly pulled off a shock victory for Zimbabwe?

6. Whose unbeaten 67 saw England defeat the West Indies in their second match in Group B?

7. West Indies's 360-4 against Sri Lanka was a new tournament record. Whose 181 off 125 balls was also the highest score in World Cup history?

8. England defeated the Windies a second time to send them crashing out of the tournament at the group stage. Whose 92 won him man of the match in that game?

9. Who took the first hat-trick in World Cup history for India when he bowed Ken Rutherford, Ian Smith and Ewen Chatfield of New Zealand?

10. Where was the semi-final between Pakistan and Australia held?

11. Whose five wickets were instrumental in denying Pakistan victory in front of their home fans?

12. In which Indian city was the second semi-final between England and India held?

13. Whose 115 gave England a total of 254?

14. Who took four wickets for England as the Indian chase fell 35 runs short?

15. At which stadium was the final held?

16. Whose 75 set Australia up for a total of 253 from their 50 overs?

17. Which Australian bowler removed Mike Gatting, attempting a reverse sweep, when England were cruising at 135-2?

18. How many runs short did England fall?

19. Who was the leading wicket taker in the tournament with 18?

20. Who was leading run scorer with 471?

TMS GREATS –
GLENN McGRATH

1. Name the city in New South Wales where McGrath was born.

2. True or false. McGrath has taken more wickets than any fast bowler in history.

3. Which Aussie cricketer is credited with having spotted McGrath's talent as a young man?

4. What year did he break into the New South Wales state side?

5. Who was the New South Wales teammate who gave him his nickname 'Pigeon' for his skinny, white legs?

6. How many first-class matches had McGrath played before he was selected to play for Australia?
    a) 4
    b) 6
    c) 8

7. Who did he make his Test debut against in November 1993?

8. Who was his first wicket in Test cricket?

9. Against which team did McGrath get his first five-wicket haul in 1995?

10. Which England batsman did McGrath make an amazing catch to dismiss at Melbourne in 2002–3 off Shane Warne?

11. Against which team in 2004 did McGrath record his Test best figures of 8-24?

12. Which batsman did McGrath dismiss at Perth in 2000 for his 300th Test wicket?

13. True or false. That wicket was part of a hat-trick.

14. Against which team did McGrath score his one and only Test half century?

15. True or false. McGrath trod on a cone before the Edgbaston Ashes Test in 2005 and was forced to miss it.

16. How many wickets did McGrath take in the 2006–7 Ashes whitewash of England?
    a) 21
    b) 24
    c) 27

17. The 2007 World Cup final against which team was McGrath's last game in an Australian shirt?

18. True or false. Melbourne band TISM released a single called 'The Parable of Glenn McGrath's Haircut'.

19. Which IPL side did McGrath play for in 2008?

20. Which county did McGrath play for in 2000, taking 80 wickets at 13.21?

WORLD CUP 1992

1. In which two countries was the 1992 World Cup held?

2. What new feature was introduced into the 1992 World Cup along with coloured clothing and white balls?

3. How many teams contested it?

4. Who made their World Cup debut?

5. Who won the opening match between the two hosts?

6. Whose 91 gave England victory in their opening match v India?

7. Which South African batsman scored an undefeated 81 to defeat the nation he had represented the previous decade?

8. Who had great success as a 'pinch hitter' for New Zealand throughout the tournament?

9. Whose 4-31 rolled back the years to help England to a convincing victory over Australia?

10. Who took 4-21 to give Zimbabwe a famous nine-run victory over England in the first stage?

11. Which team topped the round-robin table after the first stage with 14 points?

12. Where was the semi-final between Pakistan and New Zealand held?

13. Whose 60 off 37 balls in that match for Pakistan announced him as one of the best young talents in world cricket?

14. Who top scored with 83 for England in their semi v South Africa?

15. How many runs did South Africa need from 13 balls to win, which after a rain delay was then recalculated so they needed to score 21 from one ball?

16. Where was the final held?

17. Whose devastating burst to remove Allan Lamb and Chris Lewis with England in the game at 141-4 helped Pakistan to their first Word Cup?

18. Who lifted the trophy in his final ODI for Pakistan?

19. Who was joint top wicket taker in the tournament with 18?

20. Whose 456 runs were the highest in the tournament?

WORLD CUP 1996

1. In which three countries was the 1996 World Cup held?

2. How many teams played in this World Cup?

3. Which three teams made their World Cup debuts?

4. Why did Australia forfeit their opening match against Sri Lanka and the West Indies do the same later?

5. Which associate nation did West Indies lose to in the group stage?

6. Who made 137 and was on the losing side as Sri Lanka chased down India's 271?

7. Who scored a then World Cup record 188 not out in South Africa's 321-2 against the UAE?

8. Why was the start of the match between New Zealand and the UAE in Faisalabad delayed?

9. Who scored 161 as South Africa defeated the Netherlands by 160 runs?

10.   Who did Sri Lanka defeat in the quarter-finals?

11.   South Africa had been unbeaten in the group stage but lost out to which team in the quarter-finals?

12.   The quarter-final defeat to India marked the final ODI for which prolific Pakistani batsman?

13.   Why was the semi-final at Eden Gardens not completed, with Sri Lanka on the verge of victory over India?

14.   Whose 4-36 saw Australia overcome the West Indies in the other semi-final in Mohali?

15.   In which stadium was the final held?

16.   Whose 74 set up Australia's first innings total of 241-7?

17.   But whose 107 saw Sri Lanka to their first World Cup and won him the man of the match trophy?

18.   Name the victorious Sri Lanka skipper who lifted the trophy.

19.   Who was the tournament's leading run scorer with 523?

20.   Who took the most wickets with 15?

WORLD CUP 1999

1. Across which five nations was the World Cup held?

2. What new concept was introduced for this World Cup?

3. Which two sides made their World Cup debuts?

4. Who scored 88 and won man of the match as England defeated the holders Sri Lanka in the opening match at Lord's?

5. Which burly Lancashire seamer took 2-25 in that match?

6. Whose surprise three-run defeat of India in the group stage at Grace Road, Leicestershire, gave them a chance of reaching the Super Sixes?

7. At which ground did Sourav Ganguly score 183 and India 373-6 in their group match v Sri Lanka?

8. Ganguly took three wickets and was man of the match again in India's next match, as they eliminated which side from the tournament at Edgbaston?

9. Which Test side missed out on qualification from Group B?

10. New Zealand beat Australia at Chelmsford thanks to an unbeaten 80 from which English-born batsman?

11. Pakistan lost only one match in the group stage. Who to?

12. Which South African all rounder picked up four player of the match awards before his side had even reached the semi-finals?

13. Which two sides were eliminated after the Super Sixes?

14. Where was the first semi-final between New Zealand and Pakistan held?

15. Whose undefeated 113 saw Pakistan cruise to a nine-wicket victory?

16. Where was the second semi-final between Australia and South Africa held?

17. In a thrilling match, who was run out in the final over to put Australia in the final?

18. Who took 4-33 and was named man of the match as Australia hammered Pakistan?

19. Who was the tournament's leading run scorer with 461?

20. Which two bowlers were the leading wicket takers with 20?

TMS GREATS – AMBROSE AND WALSH

1.   Which Caribbean island is Ambrose from?

2.   How tall is Ambrose?
      a) 6 ft 6 in
      b) 6 ft 7 in
      c) 6 ft 8 in

3.   Which recently retired bowler did Ambrose replace to make his ODI debut against Pakistan in 1988?

4.   His Test breakthrough came during the 1988 tour of England. At which ground did he take seven wickets and was awarded man of the match?

5.   Which English county signed Ambrose to play for them the following season?

6.   Who did Ambrose take 8-45 against to level the series at Bridgetown in 1990, including trapping four men lbw?

7.   Which England batsman making his first Test appearances in 1991 is Ambrose widely accepted to have demoralized and beaten, taking his wicket six times in seven innings?

8.   Who did Ambrose trap lbw first ball for the first of his six wickets as England sought to chase down 194 to win at the Queen's Park Oval in 1994, only to slide to 46 all out?

9.   What were Ambrose's figures in his magical spell at Perth where Australia fell from 85-2 to 119 all out?

10.   When did Ambrose play his last Test?

11.   Which Aussie batsman did Ambrose have a famous on-field spat with in 1995?

12.   Which great batsman reckoned Ambrose to be the best he faced, saying, 'To succeed against Curtly meant you had graduated as a Test batsman and all those hours of practice and sacrifice were worthwhile'?

13.   Which Caribbean island does Courtney Walsh hail from?

14.   Against which side did he make his Test debut in 1984?

15.   Walsh's Test best of 7-37 came against which nation in 1995?

16.   Walsh took the remarkable figures of 5-1 in an ODI against which nation in 1986?

17. Which South African batsman was his 500th Test victim in Trinidad in 2001?

18. True or false. Walsh has more not outs than any other batsman in Test history.

19. On which West Indies ground did Walsh play his last Test in 2001?

20. How many Tests did Ambrose and Walsh play in together?
    a) 74
    b) 84
    c) 94

WORLD CUP 2003

1. In which three nations was the 2003 tournament held?

2. Which nation played in the tournament for the first time?

3. Which Australian player was sent home two days after the tournament started after testing positive for a banned substance?

4. Which Zimbabwe opener struck 172 in their opening game against Namibia, the then highest score of the tournament?

5. Why were Zimbabwe awarded the points for their game against England?

6. Which England bowler's 4-29 in their defeat of Pakistan won him the man of the match award?

7. In that match, which bowler was recorded as bowling at more than 100mph, the fastest recorded delivery in history?

8. Who took 7-20 and thumped an unbeaten 34 for Australia in their narrow defeat of England, which eliminated the latter from the tournament?

9.   Which New Zealand batsman scored his highest ODI score of 134 not out as New Zealand beat their hosts South Africa on the Duckworth–Lewis method?

10.   Who bowled Canada out for 36, to condemn them to the lowest score in ODI history?

11.   What costly error did Shaun Pollock make that consigned South Africa to elimination in a rain-affected match against Sri Lanka?

12.   Which team surprisingly made it through the Super Sixes and then became the first non Test team to make the semi-finals?

13.   Whose 5-42 for Australia saw them eliminate their Antipodean rivals in the Super Sixes stage?

14.   Whose unbeaten 91 on a slow pitch in Port Elizabeth saw Australia beat Sri Lanka to reach another World Cup final?

15.   Who famously walked for Australia in that match despite being given not out?

16.   Whose 111 in the other semi-final sent India to the final?

17.   Who scored 140 not out in the final as part of Australia's mammoth 359-2 and was awarded man of the match?

18.   How many matches did Australia go unbeaten on their way to winning the trophy?

19.   What did Henry Olonga and Andy Flower wear in Zimbabwe's first match in protest at 'the death of democracy' in Zimbabwe?

20.   Chaminda Vaas took a hat-trick for Sri Lanka in that World Cup. Who took one for Australia against Kenya?

WORLD CUP 2007

1. Where was the tournament held?

2. How many teams competed?

3. Name the three teams playing in their first World Cup.

4. Which major team failed to get out of Group B after losing to Bangladesh?

5. Whose four wickets for Bangladesh in that match won him the man of the match award?

6. Which side broke the record for highest total in a World Cup when they scored 413 for 5 against Bermuda?

7. Name the corpulent Bermudan spinner whose 10 overs for 96 in that match were among the most expensive in World Cup history.

8. Who was the unfortunate Netherlands bowler who was smashed for six sixes in an over by Herschelle Gibbs?

9. Which associate nation qualified second out of Group D behind West Indies and ahead of Pakistan?

10. Who were the only team to emerge from the 'Super 8' stage unbeaten?

11. Who took a hat-trick for Sri Lanka in their Super 8 defeat to South Africa?

12. Name the England keeper whose 52 almost pulled off a thrilling win against Sri Lanka.

13. The defeat by England in the Super 8 stage by England was which West Indies player's final international match?

14. Which future England international was in the Ireland team that went out in the Super 8 stage?

15. Whose 115 saw Sri Lanka ease past New Zealand into the final?

16. Whose 4-39 for Australia saw them bundle South Africa out for 149 and helped them cruise to the final?

17. Where was the 2007 World Cup final held?

18. Whose match-winning 149 for Australia is the highest score in a World Cup final?

19. That match marked the last of which great Australian bowler?

20. Who was the tournament's leading run scorer with 658?

WORLD CUP 2011

1. The 2011 World Cup was held in India, Sri Lanka and which other nation?

2. How many teams took part?

3. Name the elephant who was the official 2011 World Cup mascot.

4. How many groups were the teams divided into?

5. Whose 175 for India in the tournament's opening match against Bangladesh gave them a crushing victory?

6. England tied their match with India after scoring 338, their highest World Cup total. Who scored 158 for them?

7. Who smashed the fastest hundred in World Cup history in only 50 balls to give Ireland a stunning victory over England?

8. Which Ireland batsman had played for England in the 2007 World Cup?

9. Which England seamer's 4-15 helped them to a narrow six-run victory over South Africa?

10. Australia's defeat to Pakistan in the group stage ended their winning run of how many World Cup matches?

11. Whose 4-30 helped skittle the West Indies and saw Pakistan ease into the semi-finals with a ten-wicket win?

12. Which team knocked England out with an easy ten-wicket win?

13. Who defeated Australia to make sure they wouldn't win the trophy for a fourth consecutive time?

14. Who was man of the match as India defeated Pakistan in a momentous semi-final in Mohali?

15. New Zealand were defeated by Sri Lanka in the second semi-final. This defeat meant they had lost how many World Cup semi-finals?
    a) 4
    b) 5
    c) 6

16. At what stadium was the 2011 World Cup final held?

17. Who scored a hundred as Sri Lanka set India 275 to win?

18. Whose undefeated 91 saw his side to their first World Cup victory since 1983?

19. Which Sri Lankan was the tournament's leading run scorer with 500?

20. Which two bowlers claimed the most wickets with 21?

TMS GREATS –
THE WAUGHS

1. Who was born first of the Waugh twins, Steve or Mark?

2. Which state side did both play for?

3. When did Steve make his Test debut?

4. What number did he bat?

5. Which Indian all rounder was his first Test wicket?

6. Which English county did Steve play for in 1987 and 1988?

7. At which English ground did Steve score his maiden Test ton in 1989?

8. Who did his Test best of 200 come against in 1995?

9. In what year did he replace Mark Taylor as Test captain?

10. Which player did Steve choose to drop in only his forth Test in charge?

11. Who did Steve collide with on the pitch while fielding, breaking his own nose and his teammate's leg?

12. Under Steve, how many matches did Australia win consecutively in the record-breaking streak between 1999 and 2001?
    a) 14
    b) 15
    c) 16

13. True or false. Mark scored a century on debut against England in 1991.

14. Who did Mark's highest Test score of 153 come against in 1998?

15. With whom did Mark share a double-century stand at the 1996 World Cup, the first in its history?

16. Who did Mark take his best Test bowling figures of 5-40 against at Adelaide in 1995?

17. Which English county did Mark play for between 1988 and 2002?

18. Which England spinner did Mark Waugh describe as a 'fairly weak sort of player' before the 1997 Ashes?

19. During the 2001 Ashes, whose then record of 157 catches did Mark beat?

20. When did Mark retire from Test cricket?

WORLD CUP 2015

1.   In which two countries was the 2015 Cricket World Cup held?

2.   Which nation made their debut in the tournament?

3.   England lost their opening group match to Australia despite an unbeaten 98 by which batsman?

4.   Which New Zealand batsman hit a six to claim a thrilling one-wicket victory over Australia in the group stage?

5.   Who hit a World Cup record 215 against Zimbabwe on 24 February?

6.   Which batsman exceeded that less than a month later when he hit 237 against the West Indies?

7.   What record did Australia break when they totalled 417-6 against Afghanistan in Perth?

8.   Defeat by which team saw England crash out of the tournament in the group stage?

9.   Which part-time off spinner became the latest player to take a World Cup hat-trick against Sri Lanka at Sydney?

10. Whose 42 off 13 balls for the West Indies against Pakistan in Christchurch marked the second highest strike rate in an innings in World Cup history?

11. Whose 4-26 for South Africa eliminated Sri Lanka in the semi-finals?

12. Whose four wickets for Australia saw them defeat Pakistan and reach the semi-finals?

13. With five needed off two balls against South Africa, who smashed a six to take New Zealand to their first World Cup final?

14. Whose 105 set up Australia's semi-final win over India?

15. Where was the final between Australia and New Zealand held?

16. Which English umpire officiated in the final?

17. Whose three wickets for Australia earned him the man of the match award?

18. How many World Cups have Australia won?

19. Who was the tournament's leading run scorer with 547 runs?

20. Which two left armers were its joint leading wicket takers with 22?

WORLD T20 2007–9

1. When was the inaugural World T20 held?

2. Where was that tournament held?

3. How many teams took part?

4. Which batsman became the first man to hit a century in a T20 international, against South Africa?

5. Which team registered the highest T20 score by any side with 260 against Kenya?

6. How was the tie between India and Pakistan decided?

7. In the Super 8 clash against Bangladesh, who took the first ever T20 international hat-trick?

8. Who was man of the match with 70 off 30 balls for India as they beat Australia to reach a final with Pakistan?

9. Which side won the final?

10. Who was man of the match with a spell of 3-16?

11. Which nation hosted the 2009 World T20?

12. Three grounds were used to host the tournament: Lord's, the Oval and which other ground?

13. Who did England lose their first group match to in the gloom at Lord's?

14. Which one of Sri Lanka, West Indies and Australia failed to get out of Group C?

15. Which team eliminated England in a rain-affected match and reached the semi-finals?

16. Which Pakistani bowler became the first to take five wickets in a T20 international against New Zealand in the Super 8s?

17. Which Pakistani player smashed 51 and took two wickets to give his side a seven-run victory over South Africa in the first semi-final?

18. Whose 96 not out gave Sri Lanka victory over the West Indies to make the final?

19. Who won the final?

20. Which Indian batsman hit the most sixes in the tournament with nine?

WORLD T20 2010–12

1. Why was the World T20 held in 2010 and not 2011?

2. Where was it held?

3. What happened in the final over of Australia's innings in their group game against Pakistan?

4. Who became the first Indian to hit a century in a T20 international in their group win over South Africa?

5. True or false. England qualified from their group without winning a match.

6. Whose 3-23 helped assure England of their semi-final place by beating South Africa?

7. Who did England defeat in the semi-final?

8. Whose unbeaten 60 booked Australia's place in the final?

9. Who was England's man of the match with 63 as they chased down 147 to win the tournament?

10. Which England player was named player of the tournament?

11. Where was the 2012 tournament held?

12. How many teams entered?

13. Which team made their debut in the tournament?

14. Who took 4-12 as England were bowled out for 80 by India, their lowest T20 score?

15. Who's 6-8 for Sri Lanka in their defeat of Zimbabwe remain the best figures in international T20 history?

16. Whose 123 for New Zealand v Bangladesh is the highest score in the history of the World T20?

17. Who did host nation Sri Lanka defeat to reach the final?

18. Whose 75 off 41 balls was enough to give West Indies victory against Australia in the second semi-final?

19. Who won the final?

20. Which Australian scored the most runs in the tournament with 249?

TMS GREATS –
BRIAN LARA

1. On which Caribbean Island was Lara born?

2. In what year was he born?

3. True or false. He is the only player to score a hundred, double, triple, quadruple and quintuple hundred in his career.

4. Which West Indies Test player was a childhood coach and mentor to Lara?

5. In what year did Lara make his first-class debut against the Leeward Islands?

6. In his second match he scored 92 against against which island, featuring an attack led by Joel Garner and Malcolm Marshall?

7. Who did Lara make his Test debut against in 1990?

8. Lara's maiden Test century came against Australia in Sydney in January 1993 in his fifth Test. How many did he score?

9. True or false. Lara named his daughter Sydney because of that innings.

10. What year did Lara score both his 375 not against England, then the highest ever Test score, and 501 not out for Warwickshire, the highest score in first-class history?

11. Who broke Lara's record of 375?

12. When Lara reclaimed the record by scoring 400 not out v England in 2004, it made him only the second Test player to score two triple centuries. Who was the first?

13. What record did Lara hold until it was broken by Sachin Tendulkar in 2008?

14. When was Lara made West Indies captain?

15. Lara's 153 not out at Bridgetown in 1999 to help the Windies to chase 311 to win by one wicket is widely regarded as one of the best Test innings ever, and the best 'chasing' innings of all time. Who were the opposition?

16. Who did Lara make his highest ODI score of 169 against in 1995?

17. Which Durham bowler did Lara hit for four to bring up his 501 at Edgbaston in 1994?

18. What record does Lara share with Australian George Bailey?

19. True or false. Lara scored a century against every Test team bar Zimbabwe.

20. Who did Lara play his last Test against in December 2006?

WORLD T20 2014

1. Who hosted the 2014 World T20?

2. The number of teams entering the tournament increased from 12 to what number?

3. Two teams were appearing in a major international tournament for the first time. Hong Kong were one. Who were the other?

4. Which associate nation defeated Bangladesh in the group stages?

5. Name the England captain who was fined for criticizing the umpires for playing through a thunderstorm as England lost on the D/L method to New Zealand in their opening match.

6. Sri Lanka bowled which side out for 39, the lowest total by any team in an international T20 match?

7. England defeated Sri Lanka thanks to the highest score by an England player in a T20 international. Who scored it?

8. Which New Zealand player became the first batsman to reach 2000 runs in T20 internationals during his 65 against the Netherlands?

9.   Who defeated England by three runs in a thrilling match to eliminate them from the tournament?

10.   Which side were bowled out for 60 by Sri Lanka, the lowest T20 score by any Test nation?

11.   Who won the Super 10 clash between Pakistan and India?

12.   Which Pakistani batsman scored his nation's first ever T20 hundred in the defeat of Bangladesh?

13.   Who smashed 46 off 26 balls as the West Indies scored 82 off the last five overs as they defeated Pakistan to reach the semi-finals?

14.   Whose 2-5 from two overs helped Sri Lanka reach their third World T20 final by beating the West Indies?

15.   Who scored an unbeaten 72 as India chased down South Africa's 172 with five balls to spare in the other semi-final?

16.   In which city was the final held?

17.   Who won the final?

18.   Who scored an undefeated 52 to steer Sri Lanka to victory?

19.   Who was the captain who lifted the trophy?

20.   Which Indian player was named player of the tournament?

WOMEN'S WORLD CUP

1.   True or false. The first Women's World Cup was held before the male version in 1975.

2.   Which woman scored 118 to lay the foundation for England's victory in their final match?

3.   Who were runners up?

4.   Where was the 1978 tournament held?

5.   Who won?

6.   Which Australian batter was the highest run scorer with 127?

7.   Which team went through the 1982 tournament undefeated and beat England in the final?

8.   Which prolific England batter struck a then tournament record of 391 runs to top the run-scoring table?

9.   Which batter scored an unbeaten 59 in the 1988 final, making her the tournament's highest run scorer, as Australia claimed a third consecutive win by beating England?

10. Which Australian bowler who was an instrumental part of that winning side still holds the record for the most wickets in World Cup matches (39)?

11. Who did England beat in the 1993 final at Lord's to win their second World Cup?

12. Where was the 1997 World Cup held?

13. Which Australian batter posted the highest individual ODI score of all time of 229 against Denmark in Mumbai?

14. Which prolific England batter scored 173 not out in the same tournament, the highest ODI score by an England woman?

15. Which team won the World Cup on home soil, for the first time in their history, in 2000?

16. Who hosted the 2005 tournament for the first time?

17. Whose 324 runs were instrumental in England's victory in the 2009 tournament in Australia, earning her the player of the tournament award?

18. Who won the 2013 tournament in India?

19. Which New Zealand batter scored 413 runs in the tournament and went on to win Women's ODI Cricketer of the Year?

20. Where is the 2107 tournament to be held?

TMS GREATS – RICKY PONTING

1. In what year was Ricky Ponting born?

2. Where was he born?

3. Whose record did Ponting beat by 14 days when he became the youngest man to play for Tasmania aged 17 in 1992?

4. True or false. Ponting scored a hundred on his debut.

5. In Ponting's first match against New South Wales in Sydney, which future great bowler was making his debut against him?

6. His 211 v Western Australia in 1994 was his fifth consecutive ton against them. Who is the only other batsman to have achieved the same feat in state cricket?

7. Who did Ponting make his Test debut against in December 1995?

8. What did he score in his first innings?

9. In the 1996 World Cup, Ponting became the tournament's youngest centurion when he scored 102 in Jaipur against which team?

10. Ponting was dropped for the third Test against the West Indies in 1996–7 for which player?

11. Where did Ponting score his maiden Test ton after his recall to the side in 1997?

12. What number did Ponting bat in the Australian order when he made that ton?

13. In 1998 Ponting was dropped again to make way for which left-handed batsman?

14. Against which side was Ponting recalled in 1999, scoring a century on his return?

15. Against which team did Ponting score his highest Test score of 257 at Melbourne in December 2003?

16. In what year did Ponting succeed Steve Waugh as Australian Test captain?

17. Which side did Ponting score his highest ODI score of 164 against in 2006?

18. How many Ashes series defeats did Ponting endure as captain?

19. Who did Ponting play his last Test against in December 2012?

20. Which English county did Ponting play for in 2004?

DOMESTIC ONE-DAY CRICKET

1. Who did Somerset beat in 1990 in the first round of the NatWest Trophy by 346 runs, the highest margin of victory in a domestic one-day match?

2. Who sponsored the Sunday League from its inception in 1969 to 1987?

3. In the 1974 Sunday League clash at Headingley, Middlesex were bowled out for the lowest score in English limited overs history. What was it ?

4. In 2013, which county side recorded the highest run chase in 40-over cricket history when they scored 337 to beat Sussex?

5. When did the Gillette Cup become the NatWest Trophy?

6. How many overs per side was the inaugural Gillette Cup in 1963?

7. Who were the first county side to be beaten by a minor county team, in 1973's Gillette Cup?

8. In which year was the Benson and Hedges Cup introduced?

9. How many overs a side was the first B&H competition?

10. Who were its first winners?

11. Who led the Combined Universities side that almost reached the 1989 B&H semi-final?

12. Which Leicestershire bowler took a hat-trick against Surrey in the 1974 B&H final but still ended up on the losing side?

13. Why did Brian Rose declare Somerset's innings at 1 for 0 after one over, allowing Worcestershire to score the two runs they needed to win in their B&H group game?

14. Which two umpires, who had faced each other as players in the first B&H final, officiated the last B&H final in 2002?

15. Who were the first winners of the John Player League?

16. Which former Glamorgan cricketer was the regular presenter of BBC's coverage of the JPL?

17. What year was the Twenty20 Cup introduced in England?

18. Who won the inaugural Clydesdale Bank 40 final in 2010?

INDIAN PREMIER LEAGUE

1. Which came first: the Indian Premier League or the now defunct Indian Cricket League?

2. What was the first year of the IPL?

3. Name the Indian businessman and administrator who was instrumental in its organization.

4. How many teams contested the first IPL?

5. Which Indian player attracted the highest bid in the auction before the tournament?

6. Which overseas player was the subject of the second highest bid?

7. Which England and Middlesex batsman played for the Delhi Daredevils?

8. Which New Zealand batsman scored 158 in the tournament's opening game?

9. Which side won the tournament?

10. Which Australian batsman headed the run table with 616 runs?

11. Where was the second IPL tournament held in 2009?

12. Who captained the Deccan Chargers to the title?

13. Which team did they defeat in the final?

14. Which Hampshire and England ODI player played for the Rajasthan Royals in the 2008, 2009 and 2010 tournaments?

15. What colour cap does the leading scorer in the tournament wear?

16. Who scored most runs in the 2010 tournament?

17. As of May 2016, which West Indies batsman has the record for the highest IPL score of 175, scored in 2013?

18. Which Australian is the only player to have won the tournament's most valuable player award twice?

19. Who won the 2015 IPL?

20. Who was voted the 2015 tournament's most valuable player?

TMS GREATS – SACHIN TENDULKAR

1. In what year was Tendulkar born?

2. In which Indian city was he born?

3. True or false. Tendulkar turned up at a pace-bowling academy but was told by Dennis Lillee, who was running it, to focus on his batting instead.

4. How old was Tendulkar when he made his debut for Mumbai in the Ranji Trophy and scored a century?

5. Tendulkar make his Test debut against Pakistan in which year?

6. Which pace bowler dismissed him for 15 in his first innings and hit him on the nose in a later Test?

7. At which English ground did Tendulkar become the second youngest man in history to make a Test century in 1990?

8. Which England bowler did he ease through mid-off to complete that century?

9. After his two centuries in the 1991–2 series v Australia, to which teammate did Merv Hughes comment: 'This little p**** is gonna get more runs than you'?

10. Against which team did Tendulkar score three consecutive Test centuries in 1998?

11. When did Tendulkar first take over as captain of India?

12. Who succeeded him after his resignation in 2000?

13. Against which team did Tendulkar score his highest Test score of 248 not out in December 2004?

14. How many Test wickets did Tendulkar take?

15. Who did Tendulkar score his highest total in ODIs of 200 not out against in 2010?

16. Which bowler dismissed Tendulkar the most in Tests?

17. Against whom did Tendulkar play his last Test in November 2013?

18. What did he score in his last Test innings?

19.   Which county did Tendulkar play for in 1992?

20.   Despite being only 5ft 5 inches in heights, Tendulkar used
      what weight of bat?
         a) 3lb 2oz
         b) 3lb 3oz
         c) 3lb 4oz

EXTRA HALF HOUR

TMS GREATS – MUTTIAH MURALITHARAN

1. In what year was Muralitharan born?

2. True or false. Murali began his career as a medium pacer.

3. For which Sri Lankan side did he make his debut in 1991?

4. In what year did Murali make his Test debut v Australia?

5. Who was his first Test wicket?

6. Who was captain when Murali was picked to play for Sri Lanka?

7. Umpire Darrell Hair no-balled Murali for throwing in 1995. Who was the New Zealand umpire standing in that match who didn't no ball him?

8. True or false. Hair called the no balls from square leg.

9. Murali's action was cleared after testing. He was ordered to go for further testing in what year?

10. What record did Murali achieve when he dismissed Stephen Fleming in Hamilton in 1997?

11. Against which team in 1998 did Murali take his 200th Test wicket and his career-best Test-match figures of 16-220?

12. Murali reached 300 Test wickets in December 2000. It took him 58 Tests. Who is the only bowler to have done it faster?

13. Murali took 9-51 against Zimbabwe in 2002. He might have had 10 but which fielder dropped a catch at short leg?

14. In 2004, which Australian bowler became Murali's 500th Test wicket four days after Shane Warne had reached the same landmark?

15. Later that year who did Murali overtake to become the highest wicket taker of all time?

16. Warne overtook him again, but which English batsman did Murali bowl in Kandy in 2007 to claim his 709th Test victim and pass Warne?

17. True or false. Murali had played 29 more Tests than Warne when he broke his record.

18. Which Indian player became Murali's 800th and final Test victim in his 133rd and last match in April 2011?

19. For which IPL team was Murali appointed bowling coach in 2015?

20. For which English county did Murali play four seasons between 1999 and 2007?

BORN ABROAD

Many England cricketers were born elsewhere. Name the birthplace of these players:

1. Gavin Hamilton.

2. Geraint Jones.

3. Amjad Khan.

4. Martin McCague.

5. Derek Pringle.

6. Boyd Rankin.

7. Dermot Reeve.

8. Eoin Morgan.

9. Donald Carr.

10. Kevin Pietersen.

11. Owais Shah.

12. Ted Dexter.

13. Graeme Hick.

14. Bob Woolmer.

15. Andy Caddick.

16. Adam Hollioake.

17. Andrew Strauss.

18. Phillip DeFreitas.

19. Douglas Jardine.

20. Jason Gallian.

NAME THE YEAR

Name the year these momentous cricket events happened:

1. First match at Lord's.

2. First ever Test match.

3. The Ashes were born.

4. First official County Championship season.

5. Bradman's Test debut.

6. The Bodyline series.

7. First televised match at Lord's.

8. Jim Laker takes 19 wickets in a match against Australia.

9. First broadcast of *Test Match Special*.

10. Abolishment of distinction between amateurs (gentlemen) and professionals (players).

11.   Gillette Cup starts in England.

12.   South Africa suspended from international cricket.

13.   First ever ODI played.

14.   First cricket World Cup.

15.   Kerry Packer's World Series Cricket tears the game apart.

16.   Botham's Ashes.

17.   South Africa return to international cricket.

18.   Brian Lara scores highest first-class score of all time, 501.

19.   First T20 tournament inaugurated in England.

20.   Lara scores highest Test score of all time, 400.

TMS GREATS – JACQUES KALLIS

1. In what year was Kallis born?

2. What's his middle name?

3. True or false. Kallis is the first man in cricket history to score 10,000 Test runs and take 250 wickets.

4. What year did Kallis make his first-class debut for Western Province?

5. What year did Kallis make his Test debut in Durban against England?

6. Which England bowler removed him for one in his first and only innings of that match?

7. Kallis was dropped and recalled for the fifth Test but he failed to take a wicket and scored only 7. Who got him out this time?

8. Against which team did Kallis score a maiden Test century to help his team salvage a draw in 1997?

9.   In what year did Kallis become ranked as the world's best all rounder?

10. In 2005 Kallis scored the fastest half century in Test cricket against Zimbabwe. How many balls did it take him?

11. Kallis's best Test bowling figures of 6-53 came during the 2003 series in England at which ground?

12. How many five-wicket hauls did he complete?
     a) 5
     b) 8
     c) 10

13. Kallis holds the record for most Test centuries and most Test runs in South African history. What fielding record does he hold?

14. Kallis scored 45 centuries in his Test career. But how many double centuries did he score?
     a) 2
     b) 4
     c) 6

15. Against which team did Kallis achieve his highest Test score of 224 in 2012?

16. Which English county did Kallis represent in 1997?

17. When did Kallis play his last Test?

18. In 2014 he played his last ODI. Against which side?

19. True or false. Kallis has a lower Test batting average but a better bowling average than Gary Sobers.

20. Of which Indian Premier League is Kallis currently coach?

THE 99 CLUB

1. Who was the first player to be dismissed for 99 in Tests in 1902 for Australia against England at Melbourne?

2. How was Hanif Mohammad dismissed on 499, then the highest first-class score of all time?

3. Which English batsman was run out trying to get the single for his maiden Test hundred against the Aussies in 1980 in the last over before tea?

4. Which England captain was caught in the slips for 99 against South Africa in 1947, the closest he came to a Test century?

5. Which England captain was dismissed for 99 twice in his Test career?

6. The Karachi Test between England and Pakistan in 1973 was remarkable for how many men being out for 99?
   a) 2
   b) 3
   c) 4

7.   Which Yorkshire opener was out for 99 against New Zealand in Auckland in 1988, the closest he came to a Test century?

8.   Which Aussie bowler said he had 'lots of fun' getting to 99 despite missing out on a first Test century against India in Mohali in 2013?

9.   Mike Atherton was run out for 99 against Australia in 1993, the closest he came to a century at which Test ground?

10. Which Indian skipper became the first Test captain to be run out for 99 against England in Nagpur in 2012?

11. Who was the Australian batsman who was run out while acting as a runner for Craig McDermott, so leaving Steve Waugh stranded on 99 against England at Perth in 1995?

12. Which English batsman was left high and dry on 99 not out in Perth in 1979 when Bob Willis nicked Geoff Dymock to slip?

13. Which South African player was denied a third Test century when Makhaya Ntini's wild slog left him stranded on 99 against Sri Lanka in 2002?

14. Which other South African all rounder was left on a similar score a year later against England at Headingley?

15. Which West Indies batsman was twice dismissed in Test matches for 99?

16. Three batsmen have been dismissed ten times in the nineties in their Test career: Steve Waugh, Sachin Tendulkar and which other?

17. Who became the only Englishman in Test history to be out for 199 against South Africa at Lord's in 2008?

18. Which Pakistani batsman became the only Test batsman to be run out for 199 against India in 2005–6?

19. Which former England batsman was run out for 199 twice playing for Nottinghamshire in the 2005 season?

20. Two players have scored 299 in Tests. One was Don Bradman. Which New Zealander was the other?

THRILLING FINISHES

1. In what year was the first tied Test in history between Australia and West Indies?

2. How many runs did Australia need from the last (eight-ball) over?

3. Which Australian captain was out off the second ball of the over?

4. Which batsman was run out off the sixth ball seeking the third run which would've won the game?

5. Who was run out attempting a single off the next ball to mean the game was tied?

6. Which West Indies fielder ran him out with a direct hit from 12 metres out with only a single stump to aim at?

7. In what year did the second tied Test between Australia and India take place?

8. Which Australian batter was hospitalized after his first innings double hundred?

9. What target were India set to win in their fourth innings?

10. How many did they require form the last over, with nine wickets down?

11. Name the tailender who was given out lbw off the fifth ball to ensure a tie.

12. Who was the Australian spin bowler who took the wicket?

13. The West Indies and Australia contested the only Test match where the winning margin was by one run in 1993 at Adelaide. Which West Indies bowler took the wicket to win that match?

14. Who was the unlucky tailender who gloved behind?

15. The only Test match where the margin was two runs was the Ashes encounter at Edgbaston in 2005. Which umpire gave Michael Kasprowicz out caught behind to give England victory?

16. Which Aussie keeper missed a stumping when Pakistan needed three to win with nine wickets down in Karachi 1994?

17. True or false. The ball went for four byes and Pakistan won.

18. Australia were on the wrong end of another one-wicket loss, this time to India in Mohali. In what year?

19. Which Indian batsman's 74, batting with a sore back, saw his side home?

20. Which all rounder saw England home to a nervy two-wicket win at Lord's against the West Indies in 2000?

TMS GREATS – KUMAR SANGAKKARA

1. In which Sri Lankan city was Sanga born?

2. In what subject was the degree that Sanga had to abandon in 1999 when his cricket career took off?

3. In what year did Sanga make his Test debut?

4. Who did he make his Test debut against?

5. Who did he make his maiden Test century against in 2001?

6. With whom did he share a 438 partnership for the second wicket against Zimbabwe in 2004?

7. As wicketkeeper what is the most dismissals he took in one Test-match innings?
    a) 5
    b) 6
    c) 7

8.   In July 2006, Sanga made his then best Test score of 287 against which country?

9.   In what year was he first ranked as the world's best batsman?

10. True or false. Sanga is the fastest man to score 8000 Test runs.

11. When did Sanga take over the Test captaincy of Sri Lanka?

12. What was Sanga's last match as captain?

13. Who succeeded him as captain?

14. Who did Sanga hit his best Test score of 319 against in 2014?

15. Who are the only other two batsmen to hit triple Test centuries for Sri Lanka?

16. In 2007 Sanga played his first season of county cricket for which county?

17. With whom did he add 624 for the third wicket in July 2006, the highest Test or first-class partnership of all time?

18. Who were the unlucky fielding team?

19. How many Test double centuries did Sanga score in his career?
     a) 7
     b) 9
     c) 11

20. Which English county did Sanga play for in 2015?

TAILENDERS

1. What's the highest Test score by a batsman batting eight or lower?
     a) 157
     b) 207
     c) 257

2. Which England number nine smashed 169 at Lord's in 2010 against Pakistan?

3. Which New Zealand wicketkeeper holds the record for the highest score by a number nine, 173?

4. How many players have scored Test centuries batting at number ten?
     a) 3
     b) 4
     c) 5

5. Name the Englishman who holds the highest score for a Test-match number 10, 117 against Australia in 1884.

6. Which South African spinner scored 108 at number 10 against Pakistan in 1998?

7. Which Bangladeshi bowler smashed 113 for Bangladesh at number ten against the West Indies in 2012?

8. Which West Indies fast bowler hit 95 at number 11 in the rain-affected match v England at Edgbaston in 2012?

9. England's highest score by a number 11 is 81, scored at Trent Bridge in 2014 against India. Name the player.

10. Which number 11 has scored the most runs in Test history?

11. Which England spinner registered four successive ducks for England v West Indies in 1984?

12. Which England seamer repeated the feat against Australia in the 1998–9 Ashes?

13. What was Phil Tufnell's highest Test score?
    a) 18
    b) 22
    c) 26

14. Which Pakistan seamer recorded five successive ducks in 2006?

15. True or false. Monty Panesar has a first-class fifty.

16. True or false. Phil Tufnell has a first-class fifty.

17. Which Northants bowler averaged 3.33 in a career between 1974 and 1986 and registered 51 ducks?

18. Which Worcestershire player holds the record for most ducks in a first-class career, 156 of them between 1930 and 1955?

19. True or false. Fred Trueman scored 95 ducks.

20. Whose 43 off 16 balls for Pakistan against England is the highest score by a number 11 in ODI history?

OVERSEAS STARS

Name the county/counties these overseas stars played for:

1. Richie Richardson.

2. Clive Lloyd.

3. Bishan Bedi.

4. Sylvester Clarke.

5. Desmond Haynes.

6. Allan Donald.

7. Ravi Shastri.

8. Saleem Malik.

9. Carl Hooper.

10. Zaheer Abbas.

11. Javed Miandad.

12.   Tony Gray.

13.   Colin Croft.

14.   Chris Cairns.

15.   Inzaman ul-Haq.

16.   Larry Gomes.

17.   Garth Le Roux.

18.   Farokh Engineer.

19.   Darren Lehmann.

20.   Ole Mortensen.

TMS GREATS – ALASTAIR COOK

1. Which school did Alastair Cook go to from the age of 13?

2. What year did Cook make his debut for Essex?

3. Against which county did he score his maiden first-class century in 2004?

4. Cook flew from the ECB Academy tour of the West Indies to make a shock Test debut against which country in 2006?

5. True or false. He scored a fifty and a hundred in his first Test?

6. At which ground did Cook score his second Test hundred and first in England in 2006 against Pakistan?

7. Which England batsman was Cook batting with when he brought up each of his first three Test hundreds?

8. Whose record did Cook beat when he became the youngest England player to score 2000 Test runs?

9. In the second Ashes Test 2009, with whom did Cook set the record for England's highest opening partnership at Lord's?

10. Against which nation in 2010 was Cook made captain for the series while the incumbent skipper Andrew Strauss was rested?

11. How many centuries did Cook score in the 2010–1 series?

12. Against which nation did Cook make his highest Test score of 294 in 2011?

13. When did Cook take over the England captaincy?

14. True or false. He scored a century in each of his first three Tests as captain.

15. What record did Cook break in Kolkata against India in December 2012?

16. Cook's England defeated India in that series, making him the first England captain to win a Test series in India since which man?

17. Who is Cook's sole Test victim as a bowler?

18. Who replaced Cook as England ODI captain in 2014?

19. Who did Cook score a century against in 2015, his first Test hundred since 2013?

20. Whose Test record did Cook go past that year to become England's highest ever run scorer?

CLOSE
OF PLAY

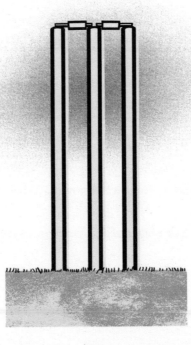

MIXED BAG

1. Which lost ground was the headquarters of Yorkshire cricket before they moved to Headingley?

2. Who was the last cricket player to win BBC Sports Personality of the Year in 2005?

3. In which year was overarm bowling deemed to be legal?

4. Who is the only fast bowler in Test history to make their debut after the age of 30 and take more than 100 wickets?

5. In which seaside town was the Central Recreation Ground, which hosted first-class cricket for a century?

6. Where is the Bourda Oval?

7. Which England spinner was known as Shaggy?

8. Who was the first player of Asian origin to play a Test for South Africa?

9. True or false. Brian Lara and Sachin Tendulkar both scored their 10,000th run in Test cricket in their 195th innings.

10. What was the name of the ground in Hull where Yorkshire played between 1899 to 1974?

11. True or false. Ben Stokes is related to famous psychic Doris Stokes.

12. Which American comedian described cricket as 'baseball on valium'?

13. How many feet does the Lord's slope drop?

14. Which Yorkshire player has a batting average of less than 2.63, the lowest of any player who has performed in more than 50 first-class games, and therefore has the right be called the worst batsman in first-class cricket history?

15. What was the name of the ground in Southampton where Hampshire played for 105 years?

16. True or false. Alec Stewart scored 8463 runs and was born on 8/4/1963.

17. What are the colours of the MCC?

18. Which club in south London, though historically in Surrey, with the initials MCC is reported to be the oldest one in the world?

19. True or false. After retiring, Somerset bowler Colin Dredge – 'The Demon of Frome' – entered the priesthood.

20. Name the stadium which was home to Darlington FC between 1883 and 2003 and also hosted Durham CC, where it was the scene of the county's first ever Championship victory in 1992.

MORE ANAGRAMS

1. Renamed Turf.

2. Unearthly Cows.

3. Towards Glue.

4. Horny Dreams.

5. Cavort Smirk.

6. Cyborg Toffee Toy.

7. Womanlike Nails.

8. Award Driven.

9. Enema Oil.

10. Leadership Fit.

11. Dawn Air.

12. Reddish Flower.

13.   Fried Mutts.

14.   Certain Worm.

15.   Callus Jerks.

16.   Be Letter.

17.   Mirage Noon.

18.   Chalkier Camel.

19.   Tricking Pony.

20.   Spartan Money.

NAME THE PLAYER 4

1. Sexual Chocolate.

2. Bunny.

3. Scooter.

4. Slasher.

5. The Slinger.

6. Funky.

7. Big Cheese.

8. A.B.

9. Jumble.

10. Jumbo.

11. Captain Cool.

12. Brigadier Block.

13.   Bingo.

14.   Tangles.

15.   Candles.

16.   Frog.

17.   FOT (Flippin' Old Tart).

18.   Bluey.

19.   Fruitfly.

20.   Human.

CRICKET OBITUARIES

1. Name the player about whom the *Daily Telegraph* said 'would have become one of the most prominent all-round cricketers ever to have played the game had his career not coincided with South Africa's years of isolation from international sport owing to the country's apartheid policy' after his death in 2015.

2. In his *Wisden* obituary in the 1974 *Almanack* who was... 'Yorkshire cricket personified in the great period of the county's domination, shrewd, dour, but quick to seize opportunity'?

3. About which colleague did Aggers say: 'Considering the years he worked as editor of *The Cricketer* magazine, and as correspondent for the BBC twice, the *Daily Telegraph* and *The Times*, and 40 years commentating on *Test Match Special* and the many books he wrote, it is doubtful that anyone has contributed more in a lifetime to the overall coverage of cricket...'

4. Who, said the *Guardian* in 2001, was 'the greatest cricketer of the 20th century and the greatest batsman who ever lived'?

5. About which fast bowler did Mike Selvey write in 1999, 'but for the sheer academia of his work, the thought he put into his performance and the skill with which he put thought into practice, no one has surpassed him'?

6. Who on his death in 2002 was described as certainly the most glamorous and arguably the most gifted of England's young cricketers'?

7. About whom did *Wisden* say in 1964: 'He extended the scope of batsmanship, added to the store of cricket that will be cherished, played the game with modesty, for all his mastery and produce, and so won fame and affection, here and at the other side of the world'?

8. Of which West Indies fast bowler was it said upon his death in 1999: 'There has never been a more feared cricketer'?

9. Upon whose death in 2015 was it said: 'A part of cricket died today'?

10. Of whom was John Arlott speaking when he said in tribute: 'The off-break is not merely the bowler's bread and butter, it is his staff of life. And in that school [he] was the past master'?

11. About whose death in military service was Donald Bradman moved to write: 'His life, his skill, his service all merited the highest honour and with great sorrow I unhesitatingly pay humble tribute to his memory'?

12. Who was Ian Botham paying tribute to in September 2015 when he said: 'None of us really expected this to happen because we thought he would probably go on until he was about 150, he was indestructible'?

13. Which great English batsman who died in 1965 was described by Neville Cardus as 'cricket in excelsis'?

14. About whom did Sir Pelham Warner say on news of his death in 1958: 'If ever there was a cricket match between England and the rest of the world and the fate of England depended upon its result, I would pick [him] as England captain every time'?

15. Which cavalier Australian cricketer when asked about death when aged 75 said: 'Never think about it. No regrets. I've had a hell of a good life. Been damned lucky'?

16. On the death of which fellow Yorkshireman in 2006 did Brian Close say in tribute: 'I captained many cricketers but none finer'?

17. On the death of which great in 1967 did J.M. Kilburn say, 'In his captaincy he won esteem and affection by the calm demeanour in which he cloaked firmness and shrewd tactics. His serenity smoothed ruffled feathers and diminished crises'?

18. To which enigmatic England bowler was Herbert Strudwick paying tribute in 1968 when he said, 'His opening delivery pitched outside the leg stump and flew over the top of the off stump. I said to a team-mate: "What sort of bowler have we here?" I soon found out. [He] could do almost anything with the ball'?

19. Which England batsman were *Wisden* describing in 1979 when they wrote, 'His technical talent matched his character and his achievements were therefore on the highest plane'?

20. Whose voice, said *The Times* after his death in 1991, 'became one of the most familiar and most mimicked in Britain, evoking the essence of both cricket and those qualities of Englishness that surround it sunny days on village greens and at country pubs and nostalgia for days gone by'?

THE FINAL TEST

1. Who scored the fastest hundred Test history in his last match in February 2016?

2. Which England player hit a four to win the match and score a Test ton in his final Test v New Zealand in 2003?

3. Who did Jacques Kallis score a ton against in his final Test in 2013?

4. Which Sri Lankan great scored a double hundred in his final Test in 2002?

5. Which much loved English batsman scored 139 in what turned out to be his last Test in Karachi in 1969 against Pakistan?

6. Which Zimbabwean hit 148 in his last Test at Trent Bridge against England in 2000?

7. Which great Australian batsman and captain struck 266 in his last Test against England at the Oval in 1934?

8. Which prolific Yorkshire and England batsman scored the last of his nine Test hundreds in his final match against Australia in 1938?

9.   Who signed off his Test career with a typically gritty 80 to ensure a draw for Australia against India in 2004?

10. Which bowler trapped Geoff Boycott lbw for six in his last Test innings against India in January 1982?

11. At which ground in England is the last Test of the summer traditionally held?

12. Hugh Trumble and Geoff Griffin achieved what feat in their final Tests?

13. After being given an ovation and three cheers from the opposition, how many runs did Jack Hobbs score in his last Test innings?
       a) 9
       b) 11
       c) 13

14. Which England fast bowler took Viv Richards's wicket for 60 in the great man's last Test at the Oval in 1991?

15. Who removed Sachin Tendulkar in his last Test innings?

16. Who was Shane Warne's last Test victim?

17. What fate befell Michael Vaughan in what turned out to be his penultimate Test innings against South Africa at Edgbaston in 2008?

18.   Who wrote the nostalgic poem 'At Lord's'?

19.   Which great spinner's career ended after a 31-year career with him taking 5-95 against the touring Australians at Scarborough on 12 September 1930?

20.   What score was Australian batsman Phil Hughes on when he was struck by a delivery which caused an injury from which he would later die?

ANSWERS

PRE-MATCH CHAT ANSWERS

WARM UP

1. Glenn McGrath

2. Quinton de Kok

3. George Davis

4. Sabina Park, Jamaica

5. Neil McKenzie

6. Steve Waugh

7. Ian Botham

8. Peter Baxter

9. 1774

10. Wilfred Rhodes

11. A bird (sparrow)

12. A falling German bomb

13. Hemmings

14. 'Soul Limbo'

15. 1957

16. Bangladesh

17. Sir Leonard Hutton

18. Graham Gooch (v Australia in 1993) and Michael Vaughan (v India in 2001)

19. A rest day

20. His bat

NAME THE GROUND 1

1. Lord's

2. Riverside Ground, Co. Durham

3. Old Trafford

4. The Oval

5. The Gabba

6. Eden Gardens, Kolkata (the first day between India and Pakistan is believed to have been watched by more than 100,000 people)

7. Headingley

8. Glamorgan

9. Melbourne Cricket Ground, Australia

10. Edgbaston

11. Seddon Park, New Zealand

12. Lord's

13. Bramall Lane, Sheffield

14. The Oval

15. Trent Bridge

16. Galle

17. Old Trafford

18. Newlands, Cape Town, South Africa

19. St Lawrence Ground, Canterbury

20. Lord's

NAME THE PLAYER I

1. Viv Richards

2. Shoaib Akhtar

3. Donald Bradman

4. Allan Donald

5. Graham Dilley

6. Ian Botham

7. Warwick Armstrong

8. Clive Lloyd

9. Phil Tufnell

10. Jack Hobbs

11. Steve Waugh

12. Sachin Tendulkar

13. David Lloyd

14. Alec Stewart

15. Joel Garner

16. Jason Gillespie

17. Rahul Dravid

18. John Crawley

19. Alastair Cook

20. Ashley Giles

NAME THE COUNTY

1. Leicestershire

2. Middlesex

3. Somerset

4. Northamptonshire

5. Lancashire

6. Somerset

7. Warwickshire

8. Yorkshire

9. Gloucestershire

10. Nottinghamshire

11. Kent

12. Hampshire

13. Yorkshire

14. Nottinghamshire

15. Kent

16. Sussex

17. Worcestershire

18. Derbyshire

19. Surrey

20. Glamorgan

QUICK FIRE 1

1. West Indies

2. Australia

3. Obstructing the field

4. South Africa and England

5. Three

6. South Africa

7. West Indies

8. *The Times*

9. 15cm

10. USA and Canada in 1844

11. Bangladesh

12. Two

13. Gary Sobers

14. Pakistan, India and Sri Lanka

15. New Zealander

16. Trevor Chappell

17. 149 not out

18. 500-1

19. King pair

20. Frank Duckworth and Tony Lewis

WELCOME TO *TEST MATCH SPECIAL* ANSWERS

NAME THE COMMENTATOR

1. Trevor Bailey

2. E.W. Swanton

3. Don Mosey

4. Mike Selvey

5. Fred Trueman

6. Henry Blofeld

7. Christopher Martin-Jenkins

8. Alison Mitchell

9. Simon Hughes

10. John Arlott

11. Brian Johnston

12. Michael Vaughan

13. Tony Cozier

14. Bill Frindall

15. Vic Marks

16. Colin Milburn

17. Phil Tufnell

18. Geoff Boycott

19. David Lloyd

20. Peter West

TRUE OR FALSE–*TMS*

1. True

2. False

3. False

4. True

5. True

6. False

7. True

8. True

9. True

10. True

11. False (she played hockey for them)

12. True

13. True

14. False

15. False

16. False

17. True

18. False (it's Bristol City)

19. True

20. True

JOHNNERS AND ARLOTT

1. True

2. Clive Lloyd

3. Don Bradman

4. Hampshire

5. Ian Botham

6. Jim Laker's 10-53 v Australia

7. 'Freaker'

8. Fred Trueman

9. Alderney

10. 1980

11. Alexander

12. *Down Your Way*

13. *Neighbours*

14. Neville Oliver

15. The Military Cross

16. 1963

17. '…stop it'

18. The coronation of Queen Elizabeth II

19. Ray Illingworth

20. 1994

AGGERS AND BOYCOTT

1. Fitzwilliam

2. Australia

3. Pinny

4. Rabbit

5. Daniel Radcliffe (Harry Potter)

6.   Greg Chappell

7.   Ed Miliband

8.   Lower

9.   Slow-scoring

10.   Leeds United

11.   Uppingham

12.   David Lloyd

13.   West Indies

14.   Gordon Greenidge

15.   100 wickets in a season

16.   He was named one of five *Wisden* Cricketers of the Year

17.   Essex

18.   Higher

19.   The 1999 Cricket World Cup

20.   Spiro (Agnew)

BEST OF BEARDERS 1

1.   False (he scored 90)

2.   True

3.   True

4. a (Afaq Hussain, Pakistan, in two tests)

5. Courtney Walsh

6. (Alan) MuLLaLLy

7. Jack Russell

8. Because he looks like one of the characters called 'Bumblies' in Michael Bentine's TV programme of that name

9. Not out

10. Australia v South Africa

11. He played the rest of his Tests for Australia

12. False, the umpires choose

13. False

14. The first batsman hits the ball into the deep; they run five including overthrows but that tally includes one short run; having crossed, the second batsman then hits a boundary

15. 1999

16. True

17. The batting side wins because the wide occurred first and therefore the match is over

18. c

19. False

20. Sydney

QUICK FIRE 2

1. 1957
2. The Third Programme (Radio 3)
3. *The Shipping Forecast*
4. Robin Martin-Jenkins
5. Middlesex
6. Eton
7. Pakistan
8. *Guardian*
9. Willie Watson
10. Foxy
11. Neil Hawke
12. Donna Symonds
13. India
14. Rugby union
15. Malcolm Ashton
16. Angus Fraser
17. Northamptonshire
18. Chelsea
19. True
20. Alan McGilvray

MEET THE TEAMS ANSWERS

ENGLAND

1. Alastair Cook

2. Jimmy Anderson

3. Len Hutton, 364

4. Jim Laker, 10-53

5. Alec Stewart

6. Alan Knott

7. Mike Atherton

8. Michael Vaughan

9. Lord's

10. 45 v Australia, 1886/87

11. K.S. Ranjitsinhji

12. Ted Dexter

13. Allan Lamb

14.   Duncan Fletcher

15.   Tony Greig

16.   North America

17.   G.L. Jessop, 76 balls v Australia in 1902

18.   Billy Bates v Australia, 1883

19.   Shakoor Rana

20.   Mike Atherton

AUSTRALIA

1.   Ricky Ponting

2.   Shane Warne

3.   Matthew Hayden (380)

4.   Arthur Mailey (9-121)

5.   Ricky Ponting and Steve Waugh

6.   Adam Gilchrist

7.   Allan Border

8.   Ricky Ponting

9.   South Africa

10.   36 v England, 1902

11.   Charles Bannerman

12. Ian Chappell with a win percentage of 50 per cent compared to Greg's 43.75 per cent

13. Keith

14. Kim Hughes

15. Keith Miller

16. David Boon

17. Shane Watson

18. Richie Benaud

19. Baggy Green

20. Bellerive Oval

INDIA

1. Sachin Tendulkar

2. Anil Kumble

3. Virender Sehwag, 319 in 2008

4. Anil Kumble, 10-74 v Pakistan, 1999

5. 200

6. Mahendra Singh Dhoni

7. M.S. Dhoni

8. 413 v New Zealand in 1956

ANSWERS

9.   England

10. 1932 v England at Lord's

11. Shikhar Dhawan

12. V.V.S. Laxman

13. Ravi Shastri

14. 24

15. New Zealand

16. Kapil Dev

17. Ajit Wadekar

18. Mohammad Azharuddin

19. Harbhajan Singh

20. Mumbai

PAKISTAN

1.   Younis Khan

2.   Wasim Akram

3.   Hanif Mohammad, 337 v West Indies, 1958

4.   Abdul Qadir, 9-56 v England, 1987

5.   Javed Miandad

6.   Wasim Bari

7. Imran Khan

8. Inzamam-ul-Haq

9. Danish Kaneria

10. 1952

11. Misbah-ul-Haq

12. India

13. Mohsin Khan

14. 2009

15. Mudassar Nazar and Javed Miandad

16. Fazal Mahmood

17. Dhaka

18. Shahid Afridi

19. Yousuf Youhana

20. Nazar Mohammad

SOUTH AFRICA

1. Jacques Kallis

2. Shaun Pollock

3. Hashim Amla, 311 v England, 2012

4.   Hugh Tayfield, 9-113 v England, 1957

5.   Graeme Smith

6.   Mark Boucher

7.   England

8.   45

9.   Lord's

10.   1970

11.   Ali Bacher

12.   West Indies

13.   Barry Richards

14.   Omar Henry

15.   Peter Pollock

16.   Abraham Benjamin

17.   Kingsmead

18.   Derbyshire

19.   Hockey

20.   Australia

WEST INDIES

1. Brian Lara

2. Courtney Walsh

3. Jack Noriega, 9-95 v India, 1971

4. 74

5. Jeffrey Dujon

6. England

7. Sir Garfield Sobers

8. Malcolm Marshall, 20.94

9. George Headley, 60.83

10. South Africa, 10.71 per cent

11. Warwickshire

12. Lance Gibbs

13. Richie Richardson

14. 'Blackwash'

15. Lawrence Rowe

16. 1950

17. Alf Valentine

18. Michael Holding

19. Chris Gayle

20. Bourda

NEW ZEALAND

1. Stephen Fleming

2. Richard Hadlee

3. Brendan McCullum, 302 v India, 2014

4. Australia

5. Stephen Fleming

6. Adam Parore

7. Martin Crowe, 17

8. 26.

9. Bert Sutcliffe

10. Chris Martin

11. Dayle Hadlee

12. Headingley

13. Nathan Astle

14. Lee Germon

15. 1930

16. West Indies

17. Lance

18. Andrew Jones

19. Black Caps

20. Wellington

SRI LANKA

1. Kumar Sangakkara

2. Muttiah Muralitharan

3. Mahela Jaywardene, 374 v South Africa, 2006

4. Rangana Herath, 9-127 v Pakistan, 2014

5. Arjuna Ranatunga

6. Prasanna Jayawardene

7. Sanith Jayasuriya, 571 v India, 1997

8. India

9. Pakistan

10. Bandula Warnapura

11. Sidath Wettimuny

12. India

13. Jayananda Warnaweera

14. Warnakulasuriya Patabendige Ushantha Joseph Chaminda Vaas

15. Marvan Atapattu

16. Kandy

17. Sanith Jayasuriya

18. Kent

19. The Lions

20. Colombo

BANGLADESH

1. Tamim Iqbal

2. Shakib Al Hasan

3. Tamim Iqbal, 206 v Pakistan, 2015

4. Taijul Islam

5. Mushfiqur Rahim

6. Sri Lanka

7. 21

8. Zimbabwe

9.   The Tigers

10. Dav Whatmore

11. Tamim Iqbal

12. Shakib Al Hasan

13. Mehrab Hossain

14. Shakib Al Hasan

15. Abdur Razzak

16. Mashrafe Mortaza

17. Mohammad Ashraful

18. Habibul Bashar

19. Kaled Mashud

20. Mushfiqur Rahim

ZIMBABWE

1.   Andy Flower

2.   Heath Streak

3.   David Houghton, 266 v Sri Lanka, 1994

4.   Paul Strang

5.   Alistair Campbell

6.   New Zealand

7.   1992

8.   Pakistan

9.   Essex

10.   Henry Olonga

11.   Grant Flower

12.   Charles Coventry

13.   Grant Flower

14.   Prosper Utseya

15.   Henry Olonga

16.   Ray Price

17.   Nick Price

18.   2006

19.   2011

20.   Nottinghamshire

DERBYSHIRE

1.   1871

2.   Because of poor performances

3.   1894

4.   They lost every single match

5.   1936

6.   A.W. Richardson

7.   Bill Copson

8.   Leslie Townsend

9.   Racecourse Ground

10.   Queen's Park, Chesterfield

11.   Les Jackson

12.   Kim Barnett

13.   Simon Katich

14.   Lancashire

15.   Dominic Cork

16.   They had lost fewer wickets

17.   John Wright

18.   Geoff Miller

19.   Mark Footitt

20.   Derbyshire Falcons

DURHAM

1. Yorkshire

2. 1992

3. The Racecourse Ground

4. David Graveney

5. Simon Hughes

6. Dean Jones

7. Wayne Larkins

8. Geoff Cook

9. 1995

10. 2003

11. 2005

12. Mike Hussey

13. Simon Brown

14. 2008

15. Martin Love

16. Paul Collingwood

17. Ottis Gibson

18. Chris Rushworth

19. Friends Provident Trophy

20. Durham Jets

ESSEX

1. 1895

2. Six

3. Chelmsford

4. 1979

5. Keith Fletcher

6. Johnny Douglas

7. Trevor Bailey

8. 1973

9. John Lever

10. Ken McEwan

11. Derek Pringle

12. Ray East

13. Graham Gooch

14. Peter Smith

15. Percy Perrin

16. Paul Prichard

17. Nasser Hussain

18. Surrey

19. Norbert Phillip

20. Essex Eagles

GLAMORGAN

1. 1921

2. Three

3. Taff

4. Cardiff Arms Park

5. One

6. 1948

7. Wilf Wooller

8. Rugby union

9. Johnnie Clay

10. Tony Lewis

11. Alan Jones

12. Matthew Maynard

13. Duncan Fletcher

14. Waqar Younis

15. Steve James

16. Don Shepherd

17. Four

18. Three

19. Jacques Rudolph

20. Glamorgan – there is no other name

GLOUCESTERSHIRE

1. The Grace family

2. W.G. Grace

3. None

4. Bristol

5. Cheltenham

6. Fred Grace

7. Wally Hammond

8. London County Cricket Club

9. Gilbert Jessop

10. One

11. Tom Goddard

12. Tom Graveney

13. Craig Spearman

14. Wally Hammond

15. Courtney Walsh

16. Mike Proctor

17. David Lawrence

18. Somerset

19. Jack Russell

20. Gladiators

HAMPSHIRE

1. 1895

2. Southampton

3. Two

4. 1961

5. Colin Ingleby-Mackenzie

6. Tennyson

7.   Phil Mead

8.   Roy Marshall

9.   Derek Shackleton

10. Barry Richards

11. Gordon Greenidge

12. Richard Gilliat

13. Malcolm Marshall

14. Butch White

15. Bobby Parks

16. Mark Nicholas

17. Robin Smith

18. Derbyshire

19. Steve Jefferies

20. Royals

KENT

1.   1842

2.   Middlesex

3.   The St Lawrence Ground

4.   Four

5.   Colin 'Charlie' Blythe

6.   Frank Woolley

7.   Tich

8.   300 wickets in a season (1928)

9.   Colin Cowdrey

10.   Derek Underwood

11.   Mike Denness

12.   Lancashire

13.   Alan Ealham

14.   Asif Iqbal

15.   John Shepherd

16.   T20

17.   Bill Ashdown

18.   Les Ames

19.   Sam Northeast

20.   Spitfires

LANCASHIRE

1. Red Rose

2. 1864

3. Nine

4. Archie MacLaren

5. Five

6. Peter Eckersley

7. Eddie Paynter

8. Len Hopwood

9. Brian Statham

10. The Gillette Cup

11. Jackie Bond

12. David Hughes

13. Jack Simmons

14. John Abrahams

15. Northamptonshire

16. Peter Moores

17. Glen Chapple

18. John Thomas (Johnny) Tyldesley

19. Brian Statham

20. Lancashire Lightning

LEICESTERSHIRE

1. 1879

2. Three

3. Oakham School

4. Old Trafford

5. Les Berry

6. Ewart Astill

7. Ray Illingworth

8. Chris Balderstone

9. Yorkshire

10. Graham 'Garth' McKenzie

11. Norm McVicker

12. 1975

13. Essex

14. Peter Willey

15. James Whittaker

16. Alan Mullally

17. H.D. Ackerman

18. Mark Cosgrove

19. Three

20. Foxes

MIDDLESEX

1. 1864

2. Ten

3. Gregor MacGregor

4. Pelham Warner

5. Patsy Hendren

6. Bill Edrich

7. Denis Compton

8. 1948

9. Fred Titmus

10. Mike Brearley

11. Allan Jones

12. Vincent van der Bijl

13. 1983

14. Wayne Daniel

15. John Murray

16. Gubby Allen

17. 1993

18. John Emburey

19. Kent Spitfires

20. Pink

NORTHAMPTONSHIRE

1. 1905

2. None

3. Sydney Smith

4. George Thompson

5. Nobby

6. They went 99 matches without winning

7. Peru

8. Frank Tyson

9. Raman Subba Row

10. David Larter

11. David Steele

12. Ollie

13. The Gillette Cup

14. Peter Willey

15. Neil Mallender

16. Alan Fordham

17. Mike Hussey

18. David Willey

19. Alex Wakely

20. The Northamptonshire Regiment

NOTTINGHAMSHIRE

1. 1841

2. Six

3. Trent Bridge

4. George Gunn

5. Arthur Carr

6. Bill Voce

7.   Walter Keeton

8.   Gary Sobers

9.   Clive Rice

10.   Richard Hadlee

11.   NatWest Trophy

12.   Northamptonshire

13.   Eddie Hemmings

14.   Tim Robinson

15.   Bruce French

16.   Stephen Fleming

17.   Adam Voges

18.   Andre Adams

19.   Chris Read

20.   Nottinghamshire Outlaws

SOMERSET

1.   1875

2.   None

3.   Lionel Palairet

4.   Harold Gimblett

5.   Arthur Wellard

6.   b

7.   Brian Close

8.   Joel Garner

9.   Brian Rose

10.   1979

11.   Hallam Moseley

12.   Nottinghamshire

13.   Vic Marks

14.   Ian Botham

15.   Peter Roebuck

16.   Jamie Cox

17.   Jimmy Cook

18.   Justin Langer

19.   Chris Rogers

20.   Sabres

SURREY

1. 1845

2. False

3. 1890

4. George Lohmann

5. Bobby Abel

6. Jack Hobbs

7. Alf Gover

8. Stuart Surridge

9. Alec Bedser

10. Micky Stewart

11. Intikhab Alam

12. David Thomas

13. Adam Hollioake

14. Ali Brown

15. Twenty20 Cup

16. Jack Hobbs

17. Kevin Pietersen

18. Tom Richardson

19. Gareth Batty

20. Guildford

SUSSEX

1. 1839

2. Three

3. True

4. Arundel or Horsham

5. Ranjitsinjhi

6. Ted Bowley

7. Maurice Tate

8. Jim Parks Senior and Jim Parks

9. Ken Suttle

10. The Gillette Cup

11. Ted Dexter

12. Paul Parker

13. John Barclay

14. Dermot Reeve

15. Chris Adams

16. Peter Moores

17. Mushtaq Ahmed

18. Murray Goodwin

19. Luke Wright

20. Sharks

WARWICKSHIRE

1. 1882

2. Seven

3. Swans Nest Lane, Stratford-upon-Avon

4. Frank Foster

5. An abnormally dry summer which suited their fast bowling attack

6. Eric Hollies

7. Bob Barber

8. M.J.K. Smith

9. Dennis Amiss

10. Geoff Humpage

11. Middlesex

12. Dermot Reeve

13. Asif Din

14. Brian Lara

15. Tim Munton

16. Nick Knight

17. Rikki Clarke

18. 2014

19. Jeetan Patel

20. Birmingham Bears

WORCESTERSHIRE

1. 1899

2. Five

3. Flooding

4. 'Fostershire'

5. Major Maurice Jewell

6. Fred Root

7. Don Kenyon

8. Tom Graveney

9. Jack Flavell

10. Basil D'Oliveira

11. Glenn Turner

12. Ian Botham

13. Graeme Hick

14. Phil Neale

15. Reg Perks

16. Tim Curtis

17. Tom Moody

18. Don Kenyon

19. The Pro40 League

20. Worcestershire Rapids

YORKSHIRE

1. 1863

2. A white rose

3. 32

4. Scarborough

5. Lord Hawke

6. George Hirst

7.   42 (27 and 15)

8.   Herbert Sutcliffe

9.   53

10. Hedley Verity

11. Bob Appleyard

12. Vic Wilson

13. Geoff Boycott

14. Six

15. Brian Close

16. Jim Love

17. David Byas

18. Herbert Sutcliffe

19. Andrew Gale

20. Yorkshire Vikings

MORNING SESSION ANSWERS

TMS GREATS – W.G. GRACE

1. 1848

2. Downend, Bristol

3. William Gilbert

4. Fred

5. 15

6. The Oval

7. 170 v Australia, 1886

8. Nine

9. Ten

10. Score a century before lunch

11. Eight

12. Gloucestershire

13. 1000 runs in a month

14. Doctor

15. 'The Champion'

16. 51

17. 44

18. Lawn bowls

19. London County Cricket Club

20. 1915

EARLY YEARS

1. George Parr

2. Australian Aboriginal cricket team

3. Ivo Bligh

4. South Africa

5. The Golden Age

6. 'The Demon'

7. Albert Trott

8. C. (Charles) Aubrey Smith

9. Lord Hawke

10. Victor Trumper

11. True

12.   Sir Pelham 'Plum' Warner

13.   Percy Sherwell

14.   Boxing

15.   Football

16.   The long jump

17.   Win the toss

18.   John Barton 'Bart' King

19.   St George's Ground, Port Elizabeth

20.   Sydney Barnes

THE ASHES I

1.   *Sporting Times*

2.   Ashes of a wooden bail

3.   Plum Warner

4.   England

5.   Warwick Armstrong

6.   Arthur Mailey

7.   False (they won one)

8.   The Oval

9.   Leg Theory

10. Nottinghamshire

11. Bill Bowes

12. Bill Woodfull

13. Gubby Allen

14. England won 4–1

15. True

16. 15

17. Don Bradman

18. Leonard Hutton

19. England's margin of victory, an innings and 579 runs

20. Hedley Verity

BETWEEN THE WARS

1. 1920, Australia v England

2. Two

3. Colin and Chris Cowdrey

4. The only completed innings in Test history where no batsman reached double figure

5. Arthur Gilligan

6. Sussex

7. Gambling

8. West Indies

9. Learie Constantine

10. George Headley

11. Thomas Lowry

12. 1–0 to England

13. South Africa 2–0

14. Douglas Jardine

15. C.K. Nayudu

16. Mumbai (Bombay)

17. Lala Amarnath

18. England

19. England had to catch their boat home

20. England v West Indies, 19–22 August

TMS GREATS – DON BRADMAN

1. Cootamundra, New South Wales

2. 1908

3. George

4. A cricket stump and a golf ball

5. Estate agent

6. South Australia

7. Nine

8. 18

9. Melbourne Cricket Ground

10. 'Braddles'

11. 452 not out

12. Worcestershire

13. Headingley

14. Wally Hammond

15. Hedley Verity

16. Stan McCabe

17. Arthur Morris

18. Eric Hollies

19. 99.94

20. 2001

BOYCOTT'S BATSMEN I

1. 51

2. Pudsey

ANSWERS

3. Lancashire

4. Old Trafford

5. Malcolm Nash

6. Ivon

7. Score a pair

8. Dennis

9. Worcestershire

10. Mark

11. 156

12. John Hampshire

13. Percy Holmes

14. Desmond Haynes

15. Sunil Gavaskar

16. Zaheer Abbas

17. Greg

18. India

19. Sheffield

20. 8114

454

POST-WAR CRICKET

1. India

2. Alec Bedser

3. 'The Bryclreem Boy'

4. Arsenal

5. A dentist

6. None

7. Lindsay Hassett

8. Rugby union

9. John Goddard

10. Frank Worrell, Clyde Walcott, Everton Weekes

11. Obstructing the field

12. Vinoo Mankad

13. He was the first professional to captain England

14. Tony Lock

15. Gary Sobers

16. Fazal Mahmood

17. 'Typhoon'

18. Handled the ball

19. Peter May and Colin Cowdrey

20. Peter May

AGGERS'S SEAMERS AND SWINGERS I

1. Leicestershire

2. Shane Bond

3. Colin Croft

4. Jimmy Anderson

5. Dennis Lillee

6. Sydney Barnes

7. Antigua

8. Brett Lee

9. Warwickshire

10. Graham McKenzie

11. Wasim Akram

12. Vernon Philander

13. Malcolm Marshall

14. Ezra Moseley

15. Devon Malcolm

16. Dale Steyn

17. Nottinghamshire

18. False

19. Wes Hall

20. Javagal Srinath

TMS GREATS – FRED TRUEMAN

1. Sewards

2. 'Fiery Fred'

3. 1949

4. India

5. Alec Bedser

6. Old Trafford

7. Lincoln City

8. Mr Bumper Man

9. Len Hutton

10. Three

11. Brian Statham

12. Lord's

13. Kent

14. 175

15. Colin Cowdrey

16. New Zealand

17. Derbyshire

18. *Indoor League*

19. 1974

20. 2006

QUICK FIRE 3

1. Sundries

2. Leicestershire

3. Jack Hearne

4. Stuart Broad

5. Matthew Hoggard

6. Lancashire

7. Viv Richards

8. David Shepherd

9. 'Banger'

10. Terence

11. Dylan

12. Fenner's

13. Mark Ramprakash

14. Michael Vaughan

15. Jason Gillespie

16. Wilfred Rhodes

17. Ranji Trophy

18. South Africa

19. 2008

20. Rajasthan Royals

NAME THE PLAYER 2

1. Geoff (G.G) Arnold

2. Chris Old

3. Michael Clarke

4. Darren Gough

5. Simon Hughes

6. Rod Marsh

7. Angus Fraser

8. Kevin Pietersen

9. Derek Randall

10. Peter Sleep

11. Andrew Strauss

12. Mark Taylor

13. Derek Underwood

14. Shane Watson

15. Michael Vaughan

16. Robin Smith

17. Andrew Flintoff

18. Glenn McGrath

19. Ricky Ponting

20. Mark Waugh (the forgotten Waugh...)

TUFFERS' TWIRLERS I

1. Jim Laker

2. Ellis Achong

3. George Simpson-Hayward in 1909–10

4. Keith

5. Hedley Verity

6. Glamorgan

7. Clarrie Grimmett

8.   Lance Gibbs

9.   Fred Titmus

10.   Northamptonshire

11.   Pat Pocock

12.   Chris Schofield

13.   Hugh Tayfield

14.   Mushtaq Ahmed

15.   Alok Kapali, Bangladesh

16.   Norman Gifford

17.   Daniel Vettori

18.   Middlesex

19.   Phil Carrick

20.   Roger Harper

TMS GREATS – GARY SOBERS

1.   Garfield St Aubrun Sobers

2.   Barbados

3.   17

4.   Alf Valentine

5. Pakistan

6. True

7. Swansea

8. Australia

9. True

10. South Australia

11. 57.78

12. Nottinghamshire

13. David Holford

14. Don Bradman

15. True

16. 1975

17. England

18. 20

19. Rohan Kanhai

20. Brian Lara

ONE-TEST WONDERS

1. Andy Ganteaume

2. Stuart Law

3.   Andy Lloyd

4.   Arnie Sidebottom

5.   Rodney Redmond

6.   Gavin Hamilton

7.   Darren Pattinson

8.   Fred Grace

9.   John Stephenson

10.   Alan Jones

11.   Mick Malone

12.   Simon Kerrigan

13.   C. Aubrey Smith

14.   Ken Palmer

15.   Alan Butcher

16.   Joey Benjamin

17.   Ian Blackwell

18.   Amjad Khan

19.   Bryce McGain

20.   Charles Marriott

SAMSON'S STATS I

1. Sachin Tendulkar

2. Brian Lara

3. England (between 1884 and 1892) and Australia (between 2005–6 and 2008)

4. 1 run (West Indies and Australia, 1993)

5. Rahul Dravid

6. Wasim Akram

7. John Edrich, 52 fours in 310 not out v New Zealand in 1965

8. Courtney Walsh, 43 ducks

9. Andrew Strauss, 2009–10 v South Africa

10. Carl Hooper, 49.42

11. 12

12. Mohammad Ashraful

13. Don Bradman

14. Bert Oldfield

15. Prasanna Jayawardene

16. Lillee and Marsh with 95 wickets

17. Muttiah Muralitharan

18. Tatenda Taibu, Zimbabwe

19. Ashton Agar

20. Mike Hendrick

THE ASHES 2

1. The Invincibles

2. Lindsay Hassett

3. The Oval

4. Denis Compton

5. Brian Johnston

6. Frank Tyson

7. Jim Laker

8. 2–1

9. Richie Benaud

10. Alan Davidson

11. Old Trafford

12. Peter May

13. 1–1

14. Geoff Boycott

15. Bill Lawry

16. Derek Underwood

17. John Snow

18. Ray Illingworth

19. An lbw decision

20. Seven (one match was abandoned without a ball being bowled)

TMS GREATS – SUNIL GAVASKAR

1. Mumbai

2. 0

3. West Indies

4. Doug Walters

5. True

6. John Snow

7. Old Trafford

8. 106

9. Australia

10. West Indies

11. The Oval

12. Don Bradman

13. West Indies

14. Kapil Dev

15. 34

16. Pakistan

17. First batsman to reach 10,000 Test runs

18. a

19. True

20. Somerset

IN THE FIELD

1. Eight (Ajinkya Rahane, 2015)

2. Younis Khan

3. Andrew Strauss

4. Frank Woolley

5. W.G. Grace

6. Ricky Ponting

7. Steve Waugh

8. Sanith Jayasuriya

9. Viv Richards

10. Mohammad Azharuddin

11. Wally Hammond

12. Alastair Cook

13. Jacques Kallis

14. 33, Australia v India, 1992

15. Rikki Clarke

16. Herschelle Gibbs

17. Shane Warne

18. Chris Scott

19. Four

20. Kapil Dev

TRUE OR FALSE

1. False (it's Cuthbert)

2. True

3. True

4. False

5. True

6. True

7. True

8. False

9. True

10. False

11. True

12. False (it was one)

13. False (Scotland)

14. True

15. False (Australia and Netherlands)

16. True

17. False (it was darts)

18. False (it was 29)

19. True

20. True (unless otherwise agreed by both sides before the match)

TMS GREATS – IMRAN KHAN

1. 1952

2. Lahore

3. 1971

4. None

5.   Three

6.   Tony Greig

7.   Wasim Bari

8.   Worcestershire

9.   Oxford University

10.   Australia

11.   Jeff Thomson and Michael Holding

12.   Sussex

13.   Javed Miandad

14.   Lord's

15.   Sri Lanka

16.   1987

17.   Australia

18.   1992

19.   The World Cup final of 1992

20.   Politics

SWANNY'S ALL ROUNDERS

1.   Wilfred Rhodes

2.   Graeme Swann

3.   Tony Greig

4.   Ian Botham

5.   Shakib Al Hasan

6.   Alan Davidson

7.   Imran Khan

8.   Aubrey Faulkner

9.   Richie Benaud

10.   Andrew Flintoff

11.   Imran Khan

12.   Richard Hadlee

13.   Kapil Dev

14.   Viv Richards

15.   Viv Richards

16.   Paul Collingwood

17.   Ian Botham

18.   Shahid Afridi

19.   Stuart Broad

20.   Sanith Jayasuriya

LUNCH ANSWERS

CRICKET QUOTES

1. David Lloyd

2. Shane Warne

3. Jeff Thomson

4. John Bracewell

5. Angus Fraser

6. Ian Chappell

7. Shahid Afridi

8. Richie Benaud

9. Robin Williams

10. Harold Larwood

11. Keith Miller

12. Mike Hussey

13. Don Bradman

14. Jim Laker

15. Kevin Pietersen

16. Shane Warne

17. Jacques Kallis

18. Devon Malcolm

19. Geoff Boycott

20. Bob Willis

LOOK IN THE BOOK I

1. *Beyond a Boundary*, C.L.R. James

2. Ian Botham

3. Douglas Jardine

4. Mike Brearley

5. Matt Prior

6. Frances, Phil Edmonds's wife

7. Jack Fingleton

8. Frank Keating

9. Simon Hughes

10. Ed Smith

11. *The Corridor of Certainty*

12. Henry Blofeld

13. Ted Dexter

14. Clive Lloyd

15. *Time to Declare*

16. Ricky Ponting

17. *Wisden Cricketers' Almanack*

18. Lawrence Booth

19. Michael Simkins

20. Fred Trueman

I DON'T LIKE CRICKET...

1. Roy Harper

2. *The Final Test*

3. *Outside Edge*

4. Hugo Weaving

5. Bradman

6. *Lagaan*

7. The Duckworth Lewis Method

8. Dave Stewart

9. *Fire in Babylon*

10. Kerry Packer

11. Flashman

12. *Netherland*

13. Rory Bremner

14. Booker T and the MGs

15. 10cc

16. Lou Bega

17. Sherbert

18. Mark Butcher

19. Brett Lee

20. Fred Trueman

TMS QUOTES

1. Robert Hudson

2. Jonathan Agnew

3. Henry Blofeld

4. Geoff Boycott

5. John Arlott

6. Brian Johnston

7. Phil Tufnell

8. John Arlott

9. Graeme Swann

10. John Arlott

11. Brian Johnston

12. Christopher Martin-Jenkins

13. Fred Trueman

14. Christopher Martin-Jenkins

15. David Gower

16. John Arlott

17. Jim Maxwell

18. Rex Alston

19. Henry Blofeld

20. Vic Marks

GOOGLIES

1. Bernard Bosanquet

2. Durham

3. Being the first streaker at an English cricket match

4.   (Ian) Botham and Eddie (Hemmings)

5.   A bread roll

6.   Hanif Mohammad

7.   His only delivery was a no ball that was hit for four

8.   His shirt

9.   Mark Robinson

10.   James Southerton in 1877 for England v Australia

11.   Wilfred Rhodes

12.   Eddie Paynter

13.   Graham Yallop

14.   Batted on all five days of the Test match

15.   He was picked for a match against South Africa which was ruined by the rain and he is the only Test cricketer never to have batted, bowled or dismissed anyone in the field

16.   John Traicos

17.   Martin Bicknell

18.   26

19.   Grant Flower

20.   Andrew Harris

MEN IN WHITE COATS

1. Harold Bird

2. Steve Bucknor

3. David Shepherd

4. Richard Terry

5. Zimbabwe

6. Harper

7. Frank Chester

8. Peter Willey

9. Rudi Koertzen

10. Arthur Fagg

11. Darrell Hair

12. Billy Bowden

13. Simon Taufel

14. Aleem Dar

15. Ian Gould

16. Steve Bucknor

17. Syd Buller

18. Mark Benson

19. Barrie Meyer

20. Lou Rowan

FAMILY TIES

1. Vic Richardson

2. Eric

3. Grandson

4. David Hussey

5. Ian

6. Jeff Jones

7. He was out first ball

8. Yuvraj

9. Brendan

10. Hanif

11. Cousins

12. Zimbabwe – Flowers, Rennies and Strangs

13. Steve and Mark Waugh

14. Geoff Marsh

15. Dean Headley

16. Richard

17. Pakistan (Hanif, Mushtaq, Sadiq and Wazir Mohammad)

18. Frank, George and Alec Hearne: Frank played for
    South Africa v England in Cape Town 1891–2

19. Alyssa Healy (Ian Healy)

20. Four

CRICKET TERMS I

1. A pair

2. Golden duck

3. Full toss

4. Long hop

5. Carrying the bat

6. Yorker

7. Cherry

8. Played on

9. Strangled

10. Mankad

11. Cow corner

12. Death rattle

13. Trundler

14. Chinese cut

15. Bunsen

16. Dolly

17. Doosra

18. Fishing

19. Sticky dog

20. Nelson

ANAGRAMS

1. Mike Atherton

2. Stuart Broad

3. Kevin Pietersen

4. Steve Waugh

5. Don Bradman

6. Graeme Swann

7. Phil Tufnell

8. Sunil Gavaskar

9. James Taylor

10. Ian Chappell

11. Colin Dredge

12. Andy Roberts

13. Ray Illingworth

14. Tom Graveney

15. Clive Lloyd

16. Trent Boult

17. A.B. de Villiers

18. Paul Reiffel

19. Darren Gough

20. Shaun Pollock

INITIAL IMPRESSIONS

1. Melbourne Cricket Ground

2. Western Australia Cricket Association

3. Leg Before Wicket

4. Marylebone Cricket Club

5. Indian Premier League

6. Decision Referral System

7. English Cricket Board

8.   One Day International

9.   Slow Left Arm

10.   Christopher Martin-Jenkins

11.   Vaas

12.   Botham

13.   Gower

14.   Richards

15.   Laxman

16.   Willis

17.   Compton

18.   (Ross) Taylor

19.   Worrell

20.   Broad

BEST OF BEARDERS 2

1.   Alan Jones

2.   b

3.   c

4.   a

5.   'Pommie' Mbangwa

6.   The narrowest range of totals over four innings: England 284 and 294; Australia 287 and 288

7.   Four (India 0-4 against England at Leeds, 1952)

8.   b

9.   Alec Bedser

10. Graeme Hick (1988, 1997, 2002)

11. b

12. Mike Atherton

13. Waqar Younis (1012)

14. David Gower

15. Andy Flower

16. Graeme Fowler

17. Geoff Allott

18. Mark Ramprakash

19. c (England v Australia in 1888)

20. b (Australia v England at the Oval in 1882)

THE PRESS BOX

1.   Christopher Martin-Jenkins

2.   Mike Atherton

3.   E.W. Swanton

4.   *Guardian*

5.   Jim Laker

6.   England v Australia, the Oval, 2005

7.   Bill Lawry

8.   Tony Greig

9.   Brian Johnston

10.   Derek Pringle

11.   Matthew Engel

12.   *Daily Telegraph*

13.   Gideon Haigh

14.   John Etheridge

15.   John Woodcock

16.   Tony Cozier

17.   *News of the World*

18.   Neville Cardus

19.   R.C. Robertson-Glasgow

20.   Henry Blofeld

AFTERNOON SESSION ANSWERS

TMS GREATS – IAN BOTHAM

1.   The Wirral (Heswall)

2.   Yeovil

3.   1974

4.   Andy Roberts

5.   Scunthorpe United

6.   Australia

7.   Five

8.   Pakistan

9.   Fastest man to 1000 runs and 100 wickets in Test history

10.   Duncan Fearnley

11.   208 v India, 1982

12.   Second slip

13.   West Indies

14. 12

15. Bruce Edgar

16. Australia

17. 1985

18. Pakistan

19. 1993

20. Hampshire

BOYCOTT'S BATSMEN 2

1. He hit it for four

2. Graham Thorpe

3. David Lloyd

4. Matthew Hayden

5. Leicestershire

6. Sri Lanka

7. Gloucestershire

8. Bobby Simpson

9. John Edrich

10. Adam Voges

11. Graham Smith

12. Mudassar Nazar

13. Peter Richardson (v South Africa, 1956–7)

14. Dennis Amiss

15. Ken Barrington

16. Doug Walters

17. Graham Gooch

18. Glenn Turner

19. Greg Chappell

20. Geoff Boycott

ASHES 1970s

1. Bob Massie

2. Derek Underwood

3. Keith Stackpole

4. Tony Greig

5. Lillee and Thomson

6. Mike Denness

7. Doug Walters

8. Colin Cowdrey

9. John Edrich

10.   Tony Greig

11.   Overnight vandalism of the pitch

12.   45 runs

13.   Derek Randall

14.   3–0

15.   Ian Botham

16.   Mike Brearley

17.   Graham Roope

18.   Rodney Hogg

19.   Graham Yallop

20.   Rick Darling

TMS GREATS – VIV RICHARDS

1.   Antigua

2.   1974

3.   Ian Botham and Dennis Breakwell

4.   Brian Close

5.   India

6.   192 not out

7.   Alan Turner

8.   Seven

9.   The Oval

10.   Northamptonshire

11.   Surrey

12.   1984

13.   Martin Crowe

14.   Rishton

15.   56

16.   Pakistan

17.   None

18.   Glamorgan

19.   England

20.   Smokin' Joe Frazier

ASHES 80s

1.   Australia

2.   Bob Willis

3.   Geoff Miller

4.   Eddie Hemmings

5.   Andrew Hilditch

6.   Tim Robinson

7.   David Gower

8.   Craig McDermott

9.   Wayne Phillips

10. Richard Ellison

11. Mike Gatting

12. Martin Johnson

13. Chris Broad

14. Jack Richards

15. James Whittaker

16. Peter Taylor

17. 4–0

18. 12

19. 393

20. Devon Malcolm

ASHES 1981

1.   'Botham's Ashes'

2.   Kim Hughes

3.   Terry Alderman

4.   Test cricket on a Sunday

5.   Bob Woolmer

6.   Ian Botham

7.   Paul Downton

8.   Alec Bedser

9.   John Dyson

10.   Chris Old

11.   111

12.   False (they were the second)

13.   No player from either side scored a half century in all four innings

14.   5-1

15.   Old Trafford

16.   Chris Tavaré

17.   Mike Whitney

18.   Allan Border

19.   Geoff Boycott

20.   Paul Parker

ASHES 90s

1.   Allan Lamb

2.   Terry Alderman

3.   Mike Atherton

4.   Mark Waugh

5.   Mike Atherton

6.   Keith Fletcher

7.   Shane Warne

8.   Mark Lathwell

9.   Michael Slater

10.   Mark Taylor

11.   Craig McDermott

12.   Darren Gough

13.   Nasser Hussain

14.   Steve Waugh

15.   Michael Smith

16.   Phil Tufnell

17.   3–1 Australia

18.   Alec Stewart

19.   Dean Headley

20.   Stuart MacGill

TMS GREATS – LILLEE AND THOMSON

1. Western Australia

2. England

3. John Edrich

4. 1973

5. The 1974–5 Ashes

6. 'If Thomson don't get ya, Lillee must'

7. Richie Benaud

8. Javed Miandad

9. b

10. Northamptonshire

11. New South Wales

12. Viv Richards

13. 0

14. David Lloyd

15. Perth

16. Alan Turner

17. Middlesex

18. Lillee

19.   Graham Gooch

20.   Queensland

SAMSON'S STATS 2

1.   Five (held by Bob Holland, Ajit Agarkar and Mohammad Asif jointly)

2.   Everton Weekes

3.   28

4.   Mohammad Yousuf

5.   Ben Stokes

6.   R.E. Foster

7.   Andy Flower

8.   Jason Gillespie, 201 not out v Bangladesh, 2006

9.   Alex Tudor, 99 not out v New Zealand, 1999

10.   Shane Warne, 3154

11.   A.B. de Villiers

12.   Kiran More

13.   Three (Imran Khan, Ian Botham, Shakib Al Hasan)

14.   Colombo

15.   Dominic Cork

16. George Lohmann

17. Anil Kumble

18. 49

19. Charlie Turner

20. Best strike rate in Test history (3.8)

ASHES 2000s

1. 4–1 Australia

2. Alec Stewart and Andy Caddick

3. Adam Gilchrist

4. Usman Afzaal

5. Michael Slater

6. Mark Butcher

7. Adam Gilchrist

8. Jimmy Ormond

9. Glenn McGrath

10. Mike Atherton

11. False

12. Simon Jones

13. 79

14. Michael Vaughan

15. Robert Key

16. Alex Tudor

17. Chris Silverwood

18. Martin Love

19. Andy Caddick

20. Richard Dawson

ASHES 2005

1. Glenn McGrath

2. Graham Thorpe

3. 17

4. Michael Clarke

5. Ashley Giles

6. Matthew Hoggard

7. Michael Kasprowicz

8. Two runs

9. His 600th Test wicket

10. Brad Hodge

11. Andrew Strauss

12. 24

13. Geraint Jones

14. Shaun Tait

15. Gary Pratt

16. Ashley Giles

17. Paul Collingwood

18. Matthew Hayden

19. 158

20. Andrew Flintoff

TMS GREATS – RICHARD HADLEE

1. Christchurch

2. Paddles

3. Canterbury

4. Pakistan

5. Both were hit for boundaries

6. 11

7. England

8. West Indies

9. None

10.   1978

11.   1000 runs and 100 wickets

12.   Middlesex

13.   Twice

14.   Clive Rice

15.   Northamptonshire

16.   Australia

17.   Ian Botham

18.   Christchurch

19.   Devon Malcolm

20.   b

AGGERS'S SEAMERS AND SWINGERS 2

1.   Peter Loader

2.   Lancashire

3.   Australia

4.   Derbyshire

5.   Richard Hadlee

6.   New Zealand

7.   b

8. New Zealand

9. Essex

10. Glenn Chapel

11. Simon Brown

12. Stuart Clark

13. Allan Donald

14. Patrick Patterson

15. Dominic Cork

16. Don Shepherd

17. Mike Atherton

18. Ottis Gibson

19. Sarfraz Nawaz

20. Jonathan Agnew

ASHES 2006–7

1. 1920–1

2. Andrew Flintoff

3. Stuart Clark

4. Alastair Cook

5. Paul Collingwood

6. Ashley Giles

7. 59-1

8. 129

9. Mike Hussey

10. Monty Panesar

11. 57

12. Geraint Jones

13. Damien Martyn

14. Andrew Symonds

15. 700 Test wickets

16. Glenn McGrath and Shane Warne

17. Andrew Flintoff

18. James Anderson

19. Justin Langer

20. Ricky Ponting

WOMEN'S CRICKET

1. Jan Brittin

2. Mary Duggan

3. Chris Matthews

4. 1934

5. England and Australia

6. Myrtle Maclagan

7. Betty Archdale

8. Rachael Heyhoe Flint

9. Kiran Baluch

10. Betty Snowball

11. A duck

12. Neetu David

13. Betty Wilson

14. Betty Wilson

15. Australia

16. England

17. Debbie Hockley

18. Charlotte Edwards

19. 1999

20. Women's Cricket Super League

ASHES 2009

1. Cardiff

2. Ricky Ponting

3. Brad Haddin

4. 69

5. Andrew Flintoff

6. Andrew Strauss

7. Peter Siddle

8. 1934

9. Shane Watson

10. Michael Clarke

11. 102

12. Peter Siddle

13. Marcus North

14. Graeme Swann and Stuart Broad

15. Ravi Bopara

16. Stuart Broad

17. Jonathan Trott

18. Ricky Ponting

19. Alastair Cook

20. Andrew Strauss

TMS GREATS – MALCOLM MARSHALL

1.   Barbados

2.   Maco

3.   False – he had only played one match

4.   Chetan Chauhan

5.   Hampshire

6.   Andy Roberts

7.   England

8.   1982

9.   India

10.   He had a broken thumb

11.   Old Trafford

12.   Graham Gooch

13.   David Gower

14.   Worcestershire

15.   True

16.   1991

17.   Graham Gooch

18.   Kent

19.   1996

20.   1999

TUFFERS' TWIRLERS 2

1.   Narendra Hirwani

2.   John Briggs

3.   Ten

4.   Tony Lock

5.   Yorkshire

6.   Bhagwat Chandrasekhar

7.   Gareth Batty

8.   Scotland

9.   Ian Salisbury

10.   Gloucestershire

11.   Phil Simmons

12.   Michael Bevan

13.   Iqbal Qasim

14.   Adil Rashid

15.   Ernest

16.   David Allan

17. Geoff Cope

18. Daniel Vettori

19. Lance Gibbs

20. None

ASHES 2010–1

1. Peter Siddle

2. Stuart Broad

3. Hobbs and Sutcliffe

4. Don Bradman

5. Simon Katich

6. The record for runs scored and minutes at the crease without being dismissed (371 runs, 1022 minutes)

7. Kevin Pietersen

8. Kevin Pietersen

9. Graeme Swann

10. Steve Smith

11. Chris Tremlett

12. Mike Hussey

13. Ryan Harris

14. 98

15. Jonathan Trott

16. True

17. Michael Beer

18. Matt Prior

19. 1986–7

20. 766

TMS GREATS – ALLAN BORDER

1. New South Wales

2. 1976

3. Gloucestershire

4. England

5. Mike Brearley

6. Pakistan

7. *Wisden* Cricketer of the Year 1982

8. Kim Hughes

9. Queensland

10. Old Trafford

11. Bob Simpson

12. The World Cup

13. New Zealand

14. West Indies

15. Be less friendly/more aggressive towards England

16. Sri Lanka

17. Courtney Walsh

18. Sunil Gavaskar

19. South Africa

20. b

ASHES 2013

1. 3–0

2. Ashton Agar

3. Stuart Broad

4. Brad Haddin

5. Jonny Bairstow

6. Joe Root

7. 1968

8. Nine

9. David Warner

10. Kevin Pietersen

11. Riverside, Co. Durham

12. Jackson Bird

13. Chris Rogers

14. Ian Bell

15. 298

16. Stuart Broad

17. Chris Woakes

18. James Faulkner

19. Bad light

20. Ryan Harris

ASHES 2013–14

1. Three

2. To avoid clashing with the World Cup

3. Nine

4. Michael Carberry

5. David Warner

6. Ben Stokes

7. Joe Root

8.   Mitchell Johnson

9.   WACA, Perth

10. Alastair Cook

11. Steve Smith

12. Mitchell Johnson

13. Graeme Swann

14. Nathan Lyon

15. Monty Panesar

16. Three

17. Boyd Rankin

18. Ben Stokes

19. True

20. Kevin Pietersen

ASHES 2015

1.   Ryan Harris

2.   Pat Cummins

3.   Brad Haddin

4.   Steve Smith

5.   Chris Rogers

6.   Adam Lyth

7.   Peter Nevill

8.   103

9.   Mitchell Johnson

10. Jimmy Anderson

11. Moeen Ali

12. Steven Finn

13. 60

14. 18.3

15. 8-15

16. Extras with 14

17. Ian Bell

18. Michael Clarke

19. Joe Root

20. Australia

BLOWER'S KEEPERS

1.   Godfrey Evans

2.   Alec Stewart

3.   Denis Lindsay

4.   b

5.   Jack Russell

6.   Wasim Bari

7.   Ridley Jacobs

8.   Bob Taylor

9.   Les Ames

10. Bob Taylor

11. b

12. David East

13. Jonathan Batty

14. Kumar Sangakkara

15. Adam Gilchrist

16. Wally Grout

17. Alan Knott

18. Ian Healy

19. Harry Martyn

20. False

TMS GREATS – WASIM AND WAQAR

1.   Lahore

2.   1985

3. New Zealand

4. b

5. New Zealand

6. Zimbabwe

7. 1992

8. 1993

9. Lancashire

10. Ricky Ponting

11. 1971

12. 1989

13. Sachin Tendulkar

14. New Zealand

15. Bowling a beamer

16. True

17. South Africa

18. New Zealand

19. Surrey

20. Bowling coach

TEA ANSWERS

VIEW FROM THE BOUNDARY

1. Lily Allen

2. 2013

3. Ed Miliband

4. Russell Crowe

5. Daniel Radcliffe

6. Elton John

7. Hugh Cornwell

8. Stephen Fry

9. Dennis Skinner

10. Archbishop Desmond Tutu

11. 1994

12. 'Underneath the Arches'

13. Viv Richards

14.   Eric Idle

15.   John Major

16.   Richie Benaud

17.   Ben Travers

18.   HRH Duke of Edinburgh

19.   Michael Parkinson

20.   Jonathan Agnew

MIDDLE NAMES

1.   Fred Trueman

2.   Ian Botham

3.   Sachin Tendulkar

4.   Brendon McCullum

5.   Alastair Cook

6.   Dale Steyn

7.   Nick Knight

8.   Steve Smith

9.   Rahul Dravid

10.   David Gower

11. Phil Edmonds

12. Robert Croft

13. David Boon

14. Mark Boucher

15. Shaun Pollock

16. Kumar Sangakkara

17. Daniel Vettori

18. David Bairstow

19. Gary Sobers

20. Mark Ramprakash

CRICKET TERMS 2

1. Plumb

2. Arm ball

3. Bump ball

4. One short

5. Fly slip

6. Hutch

7. Jaffa

8. The nets

9. (S)Nick

10. Shooter

11. Sledge

12. Wrong 'un

13. Jack

14. Spell

15. Skyer

16. Tail

17. Triggered

18. Maiden

19. Featherbed

20. Slog

LOOK IN THE BOOK 2

1. Nasser Hussain

2. Phil Tufnell

3. Richie Benaud

4. Devon Malcolm

5. Darren Gough

6. Mike Atherton

7. Duncan Fletcher

8. Glenn McGrath

9. Michael Holding

10. Graeme Swann

11. Sachin Tendulkar

12. Sunil Gavaskar

13. Allan Donald

14. David Lloyd

15. Dennis Lillee

16. Steve James

17. Alec Stewart

18. Marcus Trescothick

19. Adam Gilchrist

20. Mark Ramprakash

NAME THE PLAYER 3

1. Graham Dilley

2. Mark Ramprakash

3. Monde Zondeki

4. Trevor Bailey

5. Ashley Mallett

6. Gavin Larsen

7. Harold Bird

8. Lance Klusener

9. Keith Fletcher

10. Mark Butcher

11. Paul Reiffel

12. Colin Cowdrey

13. Virender Sehwag

14. Jonathan Agnew

15. Darren Lehmann

16. Vic Marks

17. Geoff Marsh

18. Phil DeFreitas

19. Phil Mustard

20. Mike Hussey

FOOTBALL AND CRICKET

1.   Geoff Hurst

2.   Chris Balderstone

3.   Willie Watson

4.   C.B. Fry

5.   Gillingham

6.   David Bairstow

7.   Charlton Athletic

8.   Arnie Sidebottom

9.   Brentford or QPR or Manchester City or Coventry City

10.   Phil Neale

11.   Denis Compton

12.   Alan Ramage

13.   Gary Lineker

14.   Gary and Phil Neville

15.   Tony Cottey

16.   H.E. 'Tip' Foster

17.   Viv Richards

18.   Leslie

19. Joe Gatting

20. Steve Harmison

NAME THE GROUND 2

1. Lord's

2. Headingley

3. Adelaide Oval

4. Edgbaston

5. Kensington Oval, Barbados

6. Taunton

7. New Road, Worcestershire

8. Old Trafford

9. Melbourne Cricket Ground

10. Canterbury, Kent

11. Sydney

12. Lord's

13. The Oval

14. Wankhede Stadium, Mumbai

15. Riverside, Durham

16. Sophia Gardens, Cardiff

17. The County Ground, Northampton

18. WACA, Perth

19. County Ground, Hove

20. Grace Road, Leicester

GUESS THE COACH

1. Micky Stewart

2. Peter Moores

3. Ray Illingworth

4. David Lloyd

5. Duncan Fletcher

6. Trevor Bayliss

7. Terry Jenner

8. Jason Gillespie

9. Bobby Simpson

10. Geoff Marsh

11. Dennis Waight

12. Phil Simmons

13. John Dyson

14.   Gary Kirsten

15.   Greg Chappell

16.   Tom Moody

17.   Zimbabwe

18.   Bob Woolmer

19.   Lancashire

20.   Graham Ford

BEST OF BEARDERS 3

1.   b

2.   Curtly Ambrose

3.   a

4.   Andy Caddick

5.   a

6.   False (they only have to inform them if they change their bowling arm)

7.   Anil Kumble

8.   True

9.   10-10, Hedley Verity

10.   Brian Lara

11. Denis Compton, aged 20

12. Jack Hobbs, aged 46

13. Arthur Fagg

14. A.R.L. 'Tony' Lewis

15. John Abrahams

16. Eric Hollies

17. b

18. Nottinghamshire, 1887

19. Geoff Boycott

20. True

TROUBLE AND STRIFE

1. David Gower

2. John Morris

3. Lillee and Marsh

4. Hansie Cronje

5. Shane Warne

6. Ian Botham

7. Salman Butt

8. Mohammad Azharuddin

9. Andrew Symonds

10. Andrew Flintoff

11. Mike Gatting

12. Jelly beans

13. Michael Holding

14. Chris Broad

15. Ian Chappell

16. Shahid Afridi

17. Mike Atherton

18. Mark Vermeulen

19. Ed Giddins

20. Andrew Gale

CRICKET FIRSTS

1. Sunil Gavaskar

2. Johnny Briggs

3. Charles Bannerman

4. George Giffen

5. Andy Sandham

6. Archie MacLaren

7. Fred Spofforth

8. Ned Gregory

9. Jim Laker

10. Chris Gayle

11. Charles Bannerman

12. W.G. Grace

13. Colin Cowdrey

14. Rod Marsh

15. Richard Hadlee

16. Courtney Walsh

17. Wally Hammond

18. Brian Lara

19. Sachin Tendulkar

20. Tom Horan

EVENING SESSION ANSWERS

TMS GREATS – SHANE WARNE

1. Victoria

2. Australian Rules Football

3. Accrington

4. Terry Jenner

5. One

6. Four

7. Ravi Shastri

8. Melbourne

9. 34

10. Graham Gooch

11. The most wickets ever taken by a spinner in a calendar year

12. England

13. Daryll Cullinan

14. Alec Stewart (14)

15. Devon Malcolm

16. 99

17. Hampshire

18. Rajasthan Royals

19. January 2007

20. True

SAMSON'S STATS 3

1. Sachin Tendulkar

2. Rohit Sharma

3. 443

4. 35

5. Shahid Afridi

6. Rohit Sharma

7. Misbah-ul-Haq

8. A.B. de Villiers

9. Andre Russell

10. Ian Bell

11. Jimmy Anderson

12. South Africa

13. New Zealand

14. Muttiah Muralitharan

15. Chaminda Vaas

16. Shahid Afridi

17. Joel Garner

18. Kevin O'Brien

19. Jalal-ud-Din

20. Dennis Amiss

WORLD CUP 1975

1. England

2. Prudential

3. Eight

4. East Africa and Sri Lanka

5. Dennis Amiss

6. Sunil Gavaskar

7. Glenn Turner

8. Keith Fletcher

9. Bernard Julien

10. Deryck Murray and Andy Roberts

11. Alan Turner

12. West Indies

13. Headingley

14. Gary Gilmour

15. Alvin Kallicharran

16. Roy Fredericks

17. Rohan Kanhai

18. Ian Chappell

19. Run out

20. Glenn Turner

WORLD SERIES CRICKET

1. Kerry Packer

2. Channel Nine/Nine Network

3. 1977

4. Supertests

5. Australia v West Indies

6. David Hookes

7. The batting helmet

8.   Coloured clothing

9.   West Indies

10.   Clive Lloyd

11.   Ian Chappell

12.   Viv Richards

13.   Tony Greig

14.   Wayne Daniel

15.   Asif Iqbal

16.   Alan Knott

17.   Garth Le Roux

18.   Barry Richards

19.   New Zealand

20.   1979

TMS GREATS – THE CHAPPELLS

1.   Ian

2.   Adelaide

3.   Baseball

4.   South Australia

5.   Richie Benaud

6. Lancashire

7. True

8. India

9. Bill Lawry

10. The Oval

11. Pakistan

12. 1980

13. Ian's

14. Somerset

15. Ian Redpath

16. Richie Benaud

17. Pakistan

18. New Zealand

19. a

20. The first Test batsman to score hundreds in his first and last Test innings

WORLD CUP 1979

1. England

2. 60

3.   Canada

4.   England

5.   Geoff Boycott

6.   Bob Willis

7.   Pakistan

8.   Gordon Greenidge

9.   Bruce Edgar

10.   Old Trafford

11.   Chris Old

12.   Graham Gooch

13.   Derek Randall

14.   Desmond Haynes

15.   Zaheer Abbas

16.   Gordon Greenidge

17.   Collis King

18.   Mike Brearley

19.   Joel Garner

20.   Mike Hendrick

WORLD CUP 1983

1. England and Wales

2. Zimbabwe

3. Each team played each other twice

4. Allan Lamb

5. County Ground, Taunton

6. Pakistan

7. Darren Fletcher

8. Yashpal Sharma

9. W.W. (Winston) Davis

10. Viv Richards

11. S.M. (Sandeep) Patil

12. The Oval, London

13. Javed Miandad

14. H.A. 'Larry' Gomes

15. Kris Srikkanth

16. Balwinder Sandhu

17. Kapil Dev

18. Mohinder Amarnath

19. Kapil Dev

20. Roger Binny

WORLD CUP 1987

1. India and Pakistan

2. Reliance

3. 50

4. Australia

5. David Houghton

6. Allan Lamb

7. Viv Richards

8. Graham Gooch

9. Chetan Sharma

10. Lahore

11. Craig McDermott

12. Mumbai

13. Graham Gooch

14. Eddie Hemmings

15. Eden Gardens, Kolkata

16. David Boon

17. Allan Border

18. Seven

19. Craig McDermott

20. Graham Gooch

TMS GREATS – GLENN McGRATH

1. Dubbo

2. True

3. Doug Walters

4. 1992

5. Brad McNamara

6. c

7. New Zealand

8. Chris Cairns

9. West Indies

10. Michael Vaughan

11. Pakistan

12. Brian Lara

13. True

14. New Zealand

15. False

16. a

17. Sri Lanka

18. True

19. Delhi Daredevils

20. Worcestershire

WORLD CUP 1992

1. Australia and New Zealand

2. Day-night cricket

3. Nine

4. South Africa

5. New Zealand

6. Robin Smith

7. Kepler Wessels

8. Mark Greatbatch

9. Ian Botham

10. Eddo Brandes

11. New Zealand

12. Eden Park, Auckland

13. Inzamam-ul-Haq

14. Graeme Hick

15. 22

16. Melbourne Cricket Ground

17. Wasim Akram

18. Imran Khan

19. Wasim Akram

20. Martin Crowe

WORLD CUP 1996

1. Pakistan, India and Sri Lanka

2. 12

3. Netherlands, UAE and Kenya

4. They refused to travel to Colombo due to safety concerns

5. Kenya

6. Sachin Tendulkar

7. Gary Kirsten

8. Fog

9. Andrew Hudson

10. England

11. West Indies

12. Javed Miandad

13. Rioting in the crowd

14. Shane Warne

15. Gaddafi Stadium, Lahore

16. Mark Taylor

17. Aravinda de Silva

18. Arjuna Ranatunga

19. Sachin Tendulkar

20. Anil Kumble

WORLD CUP 1999

1. England, Ireland, Wales, Scotland and the Netherlands

2. 'The Super Sixes'

3. Bangladesh and Scotland

4. Alec Stewart

5. Ian Austin

6.   Zimbabwe

7.   Taunton

8.   Sri Lanka

9.   West Indies

10.   Roger Twose

11.   Bangladesh

12.   Lance Klusener

13.   Zimbabwe and India

14.   Old Trafford

15.   Saeed Anwar

16.   Edgbaston

17.   Allan Donald

18.   Shane Warne

19.   Rahul Dravid

20.   Shane Warne and Geoff Allott

TMS GREATS – AMBROSE AND WALSH

1.   Antigua

2.   b

3. Joel Garner

4. Headingley

5. Northamptonshire

6. England

7. Graeme Hick

8. Mike Atherton

9. 7-1

10. 2000

11. Steve Waugh

12. Steve Waugh

13. Jamaica

14. Australia

15. New Zealand

16. Sri Lanka

17. Jacques Kallis

18. True

19. Sabina Park, Jamaica

20. c

WORLD CUP 2003

1.   South Africa, Zimbabwe and Kenya

2.   Namibia

3.   Shane Warne

4.   Craig Wishart

5.   England did not travel to Harare due to safety concerns

6.   Jimmy Anderson

7.   Shoaib Akhtar

8.   Andy Bichel

9.   Stephen Fleming

10. Sri Lanka

11. He miscalculated the Duckworth–Lewis total they needed to win

12. Kenya

13. Brett Lee

14. Andrew Symonds

15. Adam Gilchrist

16. Sourav Ganguly

17. Ricky Ponting

18. 11

19. Black armbands

20. Brett Lee

WORLD CUP 2007

1. West Indies

2. 16

3. Ireland, Scotland and Bermuda

4. India

5. Mashrafe Mortaza

6. India

7. Dwayne Leverock

8. Dan van Bunge

9. Ireland

10. Australia

11. Lasith Malinga

12. Paul Nixon

13. Brian Lara

14. Eoin Morgan

15. Mahela Jayawardene

16. Shaun Tait

17. Kensington Oval, Barbados

18. Adam Gilchrist

19. Glenn McGrath

20. Matthew Hayden

WORLD CUP 2011

1. Bangladesh

2. 14

3. Stumpy

4. Two groups of seven

5. Virender Sehwag

6. Andrew Strauss

7. Kevin O'Brien

8. Ed Joyce

9. Stuart Broad

10. 34

11. Shahid Afridi

12. Sri Lanka

13. India

14. Sachin Tendulkar

15. b

16. Wankhede

17. Mahela Jayawardene

18. M.S. Dhoni

19. Tillakaratne Dilshan

20. Shahid Afridi and Zaheer Khan

TMS GREATS – THE WAUGHS

1. Steve

2. New South Wales

3. 1985

4. Six

5. Ravi Shastri

6. Somerset

7. Headingley

8. West Indies

9. 1999

10.   Shane Warne

11.   Jason Gillespie

12.   c

13.   True

14.   India

15.   Steve Waugh

16.   England

17.   Essex

18.   Phil Tufnell

19.   Mark Taylor

20.   2002

WORLD CUP 2015

1.   Australia and New Zealand

2.   Afghanistan

3.   James Taylor

4.   Kane Williamson

5.   Chris Gayle

6.   Martin Guptill

7. Highest ever World Cup total

8. Bangladesh

9. J.P. Duminy

10. Andre Russell

11. Imran Tahir

12. Josh Hazlewood

13. Grant Elliott

14. Steve Smith

15. Melbourne Cricket Ground

16. Richard Kettleborough

17. James Faulkner

18. Five

19. Martin Guptill

20. Mitchell Starc and Trent Boult

WORLD T20 2007–9

1. 2007

2. South Africa

3. 12

4.   Chris Gayle

5.   Sri Lanka

6.   By a bowl out

7.   Brett Lee

8.   Yuvraj Singh

9.   India

10.   Irfan Pathan

11.   England

12.   Trent Bridge

13.   Netherlands

14.   Australia

15.   West Indies

16.   Umar Gul

17.   Shahid Afridi

18.   Tillakaratne Dilshan

19.   Pakistan

20.   Yuvraj Singh

WORLD T20 2010–12

1. To avoid a clash with the World Cup

2. West Indies

3. Five wickets fell

4. Suresh Raina

5. True

6. Ryan Sidebottom

7. Sri Lanka

8. Mike Hussey

9. Craig Kieswetter

10. Kevin Pietersen

11. Sri Lanka

12. 12

13. Afghanistan

14. Harbhajan Singh

15. Ajantha Mendis

16. Brendon McCullum

17. Pakistan

18. Chris Gayle

19.   West Indies

20.   Shane Watson

TMS GREATS – BRIAN LARA

1.   Trinidad

2.   1969

3.   True

4.   Joey Carew

5.   1989

6.   Barbados

7.   Pakistan

8.   277

9.   True

10.   1994

11.   Matthew Hayden

12.   Don Bradman

13.   Most runs in Test cricket

14.   1998

15.   Australia

16.   Sri Lanka

17.   John Morris

18.   Most runs off an over in Test match cricket (28)

19.   False, he scored centuries against them all

20.   Pakistan

WORLD T20 2014

1.   Bangladesh

2.   16

3.   Nepal

4.   Hong Kong

5.   Stuart Broad

6.   Netherlands

7.   Alex Hales (116 not out)

8.   Brendon McCullum

9.   South Africa

10.   New Zealand

11.   India

12.   Ahmed Shehzad

13.   Dwayne Bravo

14.   Lasith Malinga

15. Virat Kohli

16. Dhaka

17. Sri Lanka

18. Kumar Sangakkara

19. Lasith Malinga

20. Virat Kohli

WOMEN'S WORLD CUP

1. True. It was held in 1973

2. Enid Bakewell

3. Australia

4. India

5. Australia

6. Margaret Jennings

7. Australia

8. Jan Brittin

9. Lindsay Reeler

10. Lyn Fullston

11. New Zealand

12. India

13. Belinda Clark

14. Charlotte Edwards

15. New Zealand

16. South Africa

17. Claire Taylor

18. Australia

19. Suzie Bates

20. England

TMS GREATS – RICKY PONTING

1. 1974

2. Launceston, Tasmania

3. David Boon

4. False, he scored a half-century

5. Glenn McGrath

6. Don Bradman

7. Sri Lanka

8. 96

9.   West Indies

10.   Justin Langer

11.   Headingley

12.   Six

13.   Darren Lehmann

14.   West Indies

15.   India

16.   2004

17.   South Africa

18.   Three

19.   South Africa

20.   Somerset

DOMESTIC ONE-DAY CRICKET

1.   Devon

2.   John Player

3.   23

4.   Kent Spitfires

5.   1981

6.   65 overs

7.   Yorkshire

8.   1972

9.   55

10.   Leicestershire

11.   Mike Atherton

12.   Ken Higgs

13.   To protect their run rate so they could qualify for the next
      round

14.   John Hampshire of Yorkshire and Barry Dudleston of
      Leicestershire

15.   Lancashire

16.   Peter Walker

17.   2003

18.   Warwickshire Bears

19.   Royal London Cup

20.   Gloucestershire

INDIAN PREMIER LEAGUE

1.   Indian Cricket League

2.   2008

3.   Lalit Modi

4.   Eight

5.   M.S. Dhoni

6.   Adam Gilchrist

7.   Owais Shah

8.   Brendon McCullum

9.   Rajasthan Royals

10.   Shaun Marsh

11.   South Africa

12.   Adam Gilchrist

13.   Royal Challengers Bangalore

14.   Dimitri Mascarenhas

15.   Orange

16.   Sachin Tendulkar

17.   Chris Gayle

18.   Shane Watson

19.   Mumbai Indians

20.   Andre Russell

TMS GREATS – SACHIN TENDULKAR

1. 1973

2. Mumbai

3. True

4. 15

5. 1989

6. Waqar Younis

7. Old Trafford

8. Angus Fraser

9. Allan Border

10. Australia

11. 1996

12. Sourav Ganguly

13. Bangladesh

14. 46

15. South Africa

16. Jimmy Anderson

17. West Indies

18. 74

19. Yorkshire

20. c

EXTRA HALF HOUR ANSWERS

TMS GREATS – MUTTIAH MURALITHARAN

1. 1972

2. True

3. Tamil Union

4. 1992

5. Craig McDermott

6. Arjuna Ranatunga

7. Steve Dunne

8. False – he called them from his end when Murali was bowling

9. 1999

10. First Sri Lanka bowler to reach 100 Test wickets

11. England

12. Dennis Lillee

13. Russel Arnold

14. Michael Kasprowicz

15. Courtney Walsh

16. Paul Collingwood

17. False – he played 29 fewer

18. Pragyan Ojha

19. Sunrisers Hyderabad

20. Lancashire

BORN ABROAD

1. Scotland

2. Papua New Guinea

3. Denmark

4. Northern Ireland

5. Kenya

6. Northern Ireland

7. Hong Kong

8. Ireland

9. Germany

10. South Africa

11. Pakistan

12. Italy

13. Zimbabwe

14. India

15. New Zealand

16. Australia

17. South Africa

18. Dominica

19. India

20. Australia

NAME THE YEAR

1. 1814

2. 1877

3. 1882

4. 1890

5. 1928

6. 1932–3

7. 1938

8. 1956

9. 1957

10. 1962

11. 1963

12. 1970

13. 1971

14. 1975

15. 1977

16. 1981

17. 1991

18. 1994

19. 2003

20. 2004

TMS GREATS – JACQUES KALLIS

1. 1975

2. Henry

3. True

4.   1993

5.   1995

6.   Peter Martin

7.   Peter Martin

8.   Australia

9.   2001

10. 24

11. Headingley

12. a

13. Most catches

14. a

15. Sri Lanka

16. Middlesex

17. 2013

18. Sri Lanka

19. False – Kallis has a higher batting average while Sobers has the better bowling average

20. Kolkata Knight Riders

THE 99 CLUB

1. Clem Hill

2. Run out

3. Graham Gooch

4. Norman Yardley

5. M.J.K. Smith

6. b

7. Martyn Moxon

8. Mitchell Starc

9. Lord's

10. M.S. Dhoni

11. Mark Waugh

12. Geoff Boycott

13. Shaun Pollock

14. Andrew Hall

15. Richie Richardson

16. Rahul Dravid

17. Ian Bell

18. Younis Khan

19. Jason Gallian

20. Martin Crowe

THRILLING FINISHES

1. 1960

2. Six

3. Richie Benaud

4. Wally Grout

5. Ian Meckiff

6. Joe Solomon

7. 1986

8. Dean Jones

9. 348

10. Four

11. Maninder Singh

12. Greg Matthews

13. Courtney Walsh

14. Craig McDermott

15. Billy Bowden

16. Ian Healy

17. True

18. 2010

19. V.V.S. Laxman

20. Dominic Cork

TMS GREATS – KUMAR SANGAKKARA

1. Matale

2. Law

3. 2000

4. South Africa

5. India

6. Marvan Atapattu

7. a

8. South Africa

9. 2007

10. True

11. 2009

12. The 2011 World Cup final

13. Tillakaratne Dilshan

14. Bangladesh

15. Sanith Jayasuriya and Mahela Jayawardene

16. Warwickshire

17. Mahela Jayawardene

18. South Africa

19. c

20. Surrey

TAILENDERS

1. c – Wasim Akram

2. Stuart Broad

3. Ian Smith

4. a

5. Walter Read

6. Pat Symcox

7. Abul Hasan

8. Tino Best

9. Jimmy Anderson

10. Muttiah Muralitharan

11. Pat Pocock

12. Alan Mullally

13. b

14. Mohammad Asif

15. False

16. True

17. Jim Griffiths

18. Reg Perks

19. True

20. Shoaib Akhtar

OVERSEAS STARS

1. Yorkshire

2. Lancashire

3. Northamptonshire

4. Surrey

5. Middlesex

6. Warwickshire (though he did play a single game for Worcestershire)

7. Glamorgan

8.   Essex

9.   Kent/Lancashire

10. Gloucestershire

11. Glamorgan/Sussex

12. Surrey

13. Lancashire

14. Nottinghamshire

15. Yorkshire

16. Middlesex

17. Sussex

18. Lancashire

19. Yorkshire

20. Derbyshire

TMS GREATS – ALASTAIR COOK

1.   Bedford School

2.   2003

3.   Leicestershire

4.   India

5. True

6. Lord's

7. Paul Collingwood

8. David Gower

9. Andrew Strauss

10. Bangladesh

11. Three

12. India

13. 2012

14. True

15. Most Test centuries scored by an Englishman

16. Mike Gatting

17. Ishant Sharma

18. Eoin Morgan

19. West Indies

20. Alec Stewart

CLOSE OF PLAY
ANSWERS

MIXED BAG

1. Bramall Lane, Sheffield

2. Andrew Flintoff

3. 1864

4. Ryan Harris

5. Hastings

6. Guyana

7. Shaun Udal

8. Hashim Amla

9. True

10. The Circle

11. False

12. Robin Williams

13. Eight

14. Francis McHugh

15. The County Ground

16. True

17. Red and gold

18. Mitcham Cricket Club

19. False

20. Feethams

MORE ANAGRAMS

1. Fred Trueman

2. Courtney Walsh

3. Doug Walters

4. Rodney Marsh

5. Victor Marks

6. Geoffrey Boycott

7. Kane Williamson

8. David Warner

9. Moeen Ali

10. Phil DeFreitas

11. Ian Ward

12. Wilfred Rhodes

13. Fred Titmus

14. Martin Crowe

15. Jack Russell

16. Brett Lee

17. Eoin Morgan

18. Michael Clarke

19. Ricky Ponting

20. Monty Panesar

NAME THE PLAYER 4

1. Ryan Sidebottom

2. Graham Onions

3. Herschelle Gibbs

4. Ken Mackay

5. Lasith Malinga

6. Colin Miller

7.   Matt Prior

8.   Allan Border

9.   David Sales

10. Anil Kumble

11. M.S. Dhoni

12. Paul Collingwood

13. David Byas

14. Max Walker

15. Ray Bright

16. Martyn Moxon

17. Dennis Lillee

18. David Bairstow

19. Merv Hughes

20. Paul Romaines

CRICKET OBITUARIES

1.   Clive Rice

2.   Wilfred Rhodes

3.   Christopher Martin-Jenkins

4.   Don Bradman

5. Malcolm Marshall

6. Ben Hollioake

7. Jack Hobbs

8. Sylvester Clarke

9. Richie Benaud

10. Jim Laker

11. Hedley Verity

12. Brian Close

13. Wally Hammond

14. Douglas Jardine

15. Keith Miller

16. Fred Trueman

17. Frank Worrell

18. Sydney F. Barnes

19. Herbert Sutcliffe

20. John Arlott

THE FINAL TEST

1. Brendon McCullum

2. Nasser Hussain

3. India

4. Aravinda de Silva

5. Colin Milburn

6. Murray Goodwin

7. Bill Ponsford

8. Maurice Leyland

9. Steve Waugh

10. Madan Lal

11. The Oval

12. Hat-tricks

13. a

14. David Lawrence

15. Narsingh Deonarine

16. Andrew Flintoff

17. A golden duck

18. Francis Thompson

19. Wilfred Rhodes

20. 63 not out